hOW TO SURVIVE HOLLAND

Dealing with the Dutch
before they deal with you

HOW
TO SURViVe
hOLLAND

Martijn de Rooi
Illustrations: Jos Collignon

2007
Dutch Publishers
www.dutchpublishers.com

How to survive Holland
Dealing with the Dutch before they deal with you

Published by Dutch Publishers
Publishers Allard de Rooi, Wilbert Collet
Text Martijn de Rooi
Illustrations Jos Collignon
Design Maarten van der Kroft
Translation Tekom Vertalers, Hoofddorp
Printing Krips, Meppel
Thanks to Mike Cooper, Willem Velema

ISBN 978-90-76214-11-5
NUR 370
First printing October 2007

Trade distribution Nilsson & Lamm bv, P.O. Box 195,
1380 AD Weesp, the Netherlands. Telephone: 0294 494 949.
E-mail: info@nilsson-lamm.nl.
Business to business www.dutchshop.nl.

Dutch Publishers, Dutchshop and **Dutch Image** are registered trade names of
The Ad Agency, P.O. Box 340, 2400 AH Alphen aan den Rijn, the Netherlands.
Telephone: 0172 449 333. Fax: 0172 495 846. Internet: www.theadagency.nl.
E-mail: info@theadagency.nl.

CoNTENTS

WELCOMe IN tHE COUNTRy OF dOGSHiT

'Welcome in the country of dogshit.' These are invariably the first words uttered by a good friend of mine from Singapore on arrival in the Netherlands. He's not the only foreigner to express surprise at the habit of letting dogs out in public. Or to be baffled by the cats and rabbits which cling to his trouser leg in Dutch living rooms.

This is not a book about faeces or dogs, although the pets and the Dutch toilet – the nightmare of almost all tourists – are given the attention they deserve. Its protagonist is the *Homo neerlandicus*. He is the inhabitant of the low-lying polder kingdom of the Netherlands, which he personally conquered on the seas and transformed with exemplary diligence into a prosperous and unexpectedly multi-faceted country.

He's not a bad bloke, the Dutchman. He is informal, interested and candid, as long as you don't ask about his income. He is also tolerant, and is keen to export his ideals of freedom and equality. He is barely aware of the fact that he sometimes tramples through the global china shop with clogs on.

He's an unusual, even obstinate character, although he thinks he's perfectly normal. He's unaware that his country is brimming with sights to see and that his culture overflows with unique traditions. He's equally unaware of the fact that visitors from abroad could do with a user manual. Just catch a bus with your 'stripping card' and call around for a nice raw herring: that is his motto.

This book will guide the visitor around the mind and the kingdom of the *Homo neerlandicus*. It answers such questions as: is there a risk I will drown in the street? Who were Rembrandt and Hans Brinker? What makes Dutch football so unique? What can I do in the Netherlands and how do I get there? How can I become a fully-fledged cyclist? Why do people call the country 'Holland' and not simply 'the Netherlands'? What is Delft Blue? How can I survive Dutch cooking? Is it true I won't be arrested for lighting up a joint in the street? How come there are streets, towns and regions with Dutch names all over the world? Why do the Dutch swear by consultation and orderliness? And tulips and windmills? And are the Dutch really born skinflints?

The Netherlands, it seems, is a much more idiosyncratic and versatile country than most people think – the Dutch most of all. This guide will help the visitor to get the most out of his or her stay without drowning in the Dutch idiosyncrasies. And without slipping on dog excrement.

BaTAVIANS
ANd OTHER
bUTTERBOXES

The Netherlands for beginners

For anyone wanting to know what makes the Netherlands tick, a visit to the village of Nederland, which incidentally shares its name with the Dutch word for the Netherlands, is essential. This village in the province of Overijssel is home to a grand total of twenty-four residents, split perfectly between the two genders. If you're looking to gain an insight into the Dutch, this miniature version of Nederland (the country) is the obvious place to be. Could it be any more perfect?

Judging by the typical Dutch landscape found there, the answer is no. The village is in the De Weerribben National Park, a wetland area with international appeal. Dead-straight waterways, hundreds of ditches and breathtaking bodies of water give it the appearance of the Holland of bygone times. And the Nederlanders (those from the village) did their bit, too.

The landscape that is now admired as a nature reserve was created through the unremitting labour of its occupants, as was just about every square metre of the Netherlands. When the village of Nederland was established, the inhabitants looked out onto the expansive peat bogs that covered vast areas of the Low Countries. During the course of the Middle Ages – slightly later for the village of Nederland – these areas were exploited on a large scale.

The dried lumps of peat, known as turf, were an excellent fuel. They were transported via an intricate network of waterways to the west of the country, where even in the sixteenth century over half of the population already lived in cities; a development which only occurred in a large part of Europe three centuries later. In those parts too, a growing shortage of firewood meant that economic development was slowing down, but in what is now the Netherlands a supply of turf kept the chimneystacks puffing away.

The heavy labour involved in extracting turf left its mark on the workers from the village of Nederland – the name of the nearby hamlet of Muggenbeet ('Mosquito Bite') speaks volumes – and also on the landscape. Once the supply of peat had been exhausted, it left behind a water-rich landscape, and even complete lakes in some places. Much of this water was drained away, and some areas were granted the status of nature reserve. Without such protective measures, there would not be any 'unspoilt nature' left in the small, densely-populated and enterprising Netherlands.

The Nederlanders (the ones from the village) made a virtue of necessity in their peatless, watery landscape and turned to growing reed after 1920. The first-rate Overijssel reed was in demand as a roofing material throughout Europe. The trade has remained alive in the region, but the gradual drying-out of the land and the unstoppable rise of the roof tile compelled most of the occupants to turn their hands to farming over the course of the last century. Since then, many have also given up agriculture. The intensive existence and the long boat trips to dry land with cattle, milk churns and all has taken its toll.

For visitors to the De Weerribben National Park, the last of the 'water farmers' form part of a rural idyll, frozen in time. A reserve for reed cutters and other odd birds, where one travels by boat and where some villages have only become accessible by car in the last fifty years or so, with the 'Nederland' road sign as the jewel in the tourism crown – it is a wet, nostalgic dream. However, if you're expecting a cross-section of Dutch society you'd be better off visiting the miniature city of Madurodam in The Hague.

Even so, there is one similarity between the village and the country of the same name. It may be invisible, but that does not dilute it in any way. The country is often referred to as 'one big village' by its inhabitants, and this is entirely to do with its size. Measured from border to border, the three hundred or so kilometres between the southernmost point of the province of Limburg and the northern West-Frisian Island of Rottum is the longest distance between two points within the Netherlands.

Many foreigners think it highly amusing, a country you can travel right across in a couple of hours. And charming it indeed is, as where else today would you find towns full of history, 'coffee' shops and contemporary culture, top(less) beaches and nature reserves full of reed cutters and exceptional flora and fauna, all within a stone's throw of each other?

These village-like proportions have had a great influence on Dutch culture and manners from the very beginning. The Netherlands is not only the largest but also by far the most overcrowded village in Europe. With nearly 16.4 million inhabitants, it is one of the most densely-populated countries in the world, and that is not just something you'll discover by waiting in the queue for the supermarket checkout. Negotiation, adaptability and tolerance are dire necessities for the Dutch, with their astonishing range of backgrounds, in keeping things relatively comfortable. Even if it's just because you keep bumping into each other on the village square. In the horseshoe-shaped *Randstad* area in particular, the heavily-urbanised region in the west which encompasses Amsterdam, Rotterdam, The Hague and Utrecht, the Dutch do find themselves tripping over each other.

No one would have expected this in the least when, around the beginning of our era, the Batavians floated into the region now known as the Netherlands. These Germanic people were cherished as the forebears of the Dutch people for centuries. In primary school, where I was trained in being Dutch, teachers spoke evocatively of the bold warriors who drifted down the Rhine on tree trunks and settled in the region of the big rivers. According to the Romans, who during the same period established the Rhine as the northern border of their empire and provided the first descriptions of our region, the Batavians' bravery was what distinguished them from the motley assortment that had previously settled in the chilly, swampy land. This lot were barbarians, who staggered aimlessly around their swamps, spending their time drinking beer and gambling their women away, living on bumps in the landscape like castaways, digging up peat here and there and using the dried sludge as fuel. According to the Romans they must, therefore, be deeply unhappy people.

Oh, but the Batavians! They crossed the Rhine on horseback, whistling cheerfully away, and in full armour too. The armour was Roman, as the Batavians turned out to be loyal vassals and integrated exemplarily into the Romanised society that blossomed south of the Rhine. There the Romans introduced money, law, a calendar and their system of weights and measures, and established a network of metalled roads between the twenty Roman forts on the Rhine and the first towns, which included Heerlen, Voorburg and the Batavian 'capital' of Nijmegen.

Five thousand of an estimated forty thousand Batavians served in the Roman legions. After twenty-five years of faithful service, they returned home with their Roman passports and the latest Roman trinkets, where they started their own farms using their savings and well-earned pensions.

Apart from the tree trunks, which seemed to me a somewhat primitive mode of transport for the founding fathers of a modern civilisation, I thought as a pupil that we ought to be happy with our Batavian ancestors. Even so, the teachers' stories gave me cause for doubt. How could it be that the Batavians alone had made a contribution to the proud foundations of our fatherland, and not the barbarian turf burners – tribes with catchy names such as the Cananefates and the Menapii? Did they, perhaps, gamble all their women away, renounce procreation, or turn their backs on the boggy little region? And what about the Frisians, who according to the same teachers still occupied a large area of the country, a whole province in fact, near to the modern reserve for reed cutters? Were the Romans, perhaps, exaggerating when glorifying the Batavians?

Were those tree-trunk-tourists actually Dutch at all? Were they any good at making clogs and building dikes? According to the Romans they ate cheese, so from that perspective they deserved the benefit of the doubt. However, all things taken into account, I was on the brink of losing my faith in the Batavians.

My critical questions did not prevent the Batavians from taking on mythical proportions. They took their time with it too, until well into the sixteenth century. Under the leadership of Willem van Oranje (William of Orange), who was to become the 'Father of the Fatherland', the inhabitants of what is now the Netherlands rose in revolt against the King of Spain, who was also the ruler of the Low Countries. He had become immensely unpopular due to a series of callous measures. He encroached on the privileges of the local aristocracy and, being a fervent Catholic, attacked the rising Protestant movement without mercy.

In this situation, the proud Batavians were exhumed as role models. After all, they had made the mighty Rome look foolish in the year 69 by rebelling briefly and burning down the Roman forts along the Rhine. With this Batavian inspiration, the inhabitants took up arms against the Spanish oppressor.

The conflict with Spain took a chaotic course and would drag on for eighty years; a peace treaty was signed only in 1648. Initially, the seven insurgent regions sought a new, more agreeable ruler, but suitable candidates were thin on the ground and in 1588, for want of a better solution, they decided to become the Republic of the Seven United Netherlands. A startling move, not only because absolute sovereigns were increasingly holding way in Europe, but also because the Republic was a collaboration between independent regions without any central structure to speak of. The role of leader was assumed by the powerful province of Holland – the reason why the Netherlands is still known by that name, even though Noord- and Zuid-Holland are now only two of twelve provinces.

What was even more astounding was that the tiny Republic quickly started playing a leading part on the world stage. Building on a strong trading tradition, it grew into the first modern economy, admired by contemporaries everywhere for its prosperity and highly-developed, very progressive, civil urban culture. Large numbers of well-heeled exiles from all over Europe benefited gratefully from the relatively high freedom of conscience in the Republic. Also, the entire civilised world benefited from the freedom of the press for centuries. As such, this miraculous creation was an important first step towards two of the most significant cornerstones of western civilisation: capitalism, with its unprecedented prosperity, and the Enlightenment with its fundamental rejection of (religious) quibbling and its sacred trust in human intellect and shrewdness.

Supported by what later became known as the Batavian myth, the Republic shone throughout the Golden Age – roughly the period of 1600-1670 – in virtually every field. And the Batavians basked in reflected glory. With the prophetic words 'Something grand can be accomplished here', Jan Pieterszoon Coen founded the commercial metropolis of Batavia on the island of Java – the present-day Indonesian capital of Jakarta – on behalf of the Dutch East India Company (VOC), which was the first stock exchange-listed enterprise in the world. Rembrandt, commissioned by the city of Amsterdam, immortalised the Batavian leader Julius Civilis, who rose against the Romans. The famous poet, Joost van den Vondel, published an ode to this 'resistance hero'.

Greased with Batavian wonder oil, the superpower that was the Republic became a rich reservoir of stereotypes which are still thought of as 'typically Dutch' to the present day. The Dutch are still renowned for being enterprising, uncomplicated, sincere, rational, freedom-loving, tolerant, liberal, cosmopolitan and civil. And, let's not forget: pedantic and frugal.

And that wasn't the last word from the Batavians. During the latter days of the Republic, the call for political reforms rose from among the enlightened bourgeoisie. This 'patriotic movement' turned its back on the administrative elite, dominated by the Oranje dynasty of the Father of the Fatherland, from which it was to a great extent excluded, and against the 'moral erosion' that had taken the nation over. Basing itself on the Enlightenment ideals of liberty and equality, it called for democracy, education and development, to be realised within a strong nation state. In fact, its intention was to restore the glory of the old Republic which had had to relinquish its position of power to Britain. The patriots published pamphlets calling on 'the entire Dutch nation, descendants of the Free Batavians' to seize power.

In 1795, they proclaimed the Batavian Republic, with the support of the French, who themselves had just realised the ideal of liberty, equality and brotherhood with the help of the guillotine. What was unique was that the new state system was erected with a parliament of elected representatives and a 'Constitution of the Batavian People', the first Dutch constitution, which had some staggeringly modern features: the separation of church and state, suffrage for all citizens, freedom of speech, press and religion, and 'support for the poor', though with the exception of 'the wilfully idle'.

In this way the modern Netherlands was established and named after the Batavian tree trunk sailors. The Netherlands was soon definitively on the map as a strong, democratic, liberal constitutional state, the icing on the cake being the 1848 Constitution which, in broad outlines, is still in force today. It would form the preface to a second heyday, which became known as the Second Golden Age.

Room was set aside within this new national entity for the Oranje dynasty. Following the extraordinary republican adventure, the Netherlands ended up becoming a monarchy, officially called the Kingdom of the Netherlands. The plural in the name still refers to the independent provinces which had brought the country unprecedented prosperity.

For a while during those turbulent times it seemed that the state would also include the Belgians, its southern neighbours who were defeated by the Spanish king during the Revolt against Spain. However, despite the kinship, the gulf between the Northern and Southern Netherlands proved too great.

The connection between the two countries is characterised nowadays by mutual compliments and good-humoured banter. The Belgian, in Dutch eyes, is an incorrigible Burgundian who knows how to enjoy himself, while at the same time playing the starring role of fool in the unending series of 'Belgian jokes' with which the Dutch enthusiastically regale each other. In turn, the Dutchman is revered for his relaxed, informal lifestyle, but is also known as a surly *kaaskop* (cheese head) with an excessively big mouth. This mocking identification of the Dutch with their famed export products has a rich history all of its own. In Britain, they were known in the past as 'butterboxes'.

Once the old Republic had been consigned to history, the Batavians also lost their appeal. Their role was taken over by the new national myth: the Golden Age. From 1800, this myth had the modern, patriotically-schooled Netherlands in its grasp.

The Batavian symbolism also faded slowly but surely, ending up finally in history's scrap heap. The historical tale that my primary school teachers told so vividly only forty years ago cannot be heard in any classroom today. Modern Dutch memories of the Batavians are vague at best. Julius Civilis and his people live on anonymously in the modern name for their old region, the Betuwe, and in the names of football clubs, cafés, Indonesian restaurants and the bicycle manufacturer Batavus, which is as Dutch as it gets.

Only on special occasions the stops are pulled out once again. For example, Lelystad, capital of the province of Flevoland, splashed out with a whole series of Batavian names. And why not? The polder province was only recently won back from the wild Zuiderzee, the old inland sea on which the ships of the VOC sailed back and forth en route from Amsterdam to the distant Batavia. The most fitting tribute to this heady past is the replica of the proud VOC ship *Batavia* on Lelystad's Batavia wharf. A district also bears the name, as does a vets' practice specialising in homeopathic treatment. There is even a shopping mall called Batavia Stad, situated on the Batavia square, where customers are lured by high discounts, in the best traditions of commerce. The city itself is named after Cornelis Lely, the genius behind the partial reclamation of the inland sea, while the word 'Flevoland' revisits the Roman name for the ancient lake that was later to become the Zuiderzee.

In Lelystad, the formation of myths surrounding the Batavians blends beautifully with another heroic characteristic that forms a leitmotif through Dutch history: the everlasting battle against water. This struggle has influenced Dutch culture profoundly. Constructive cooperation was an essential requirement for keeping one's head, literally, above water.

The memory of the Batavians is also kept alive abroad, for example by the Indonesian airline Batavia Air. In the United States alone, there are numerous places with the name Batavia – one of many reminders of the Dutch influence in that country. However, there too you will find hardly anyone who knows that the Batavians disappeared through the back door of history around the year 300. They were probably swallowed up in the maelstrom of events that is referred to as the Great Migration of Peoples, the ethic centrifuge that drew peoples such as the Saxons and the Franks to the Low Countries. Until the creation of the Dutch Republic at the end of the sixteenth century, the region now known as the Netherlands was subject to the comings and goings of many guests, some welcome and some less so. The region became part of powerful empires on a number of occasions – Frankish, Burgundian, Habsburg and Spanish – while at the same time local rulers, bishops and later on, provinces and cities attempted to expand their influence.

That the Republic emerged from this long, turbulent period as an independent nation was more coincidental than planned: it was the unintentional outcome of a breathtaking complex of factors. The idea that the country had always been there, with a primeval Batavian population, and had been laid down to mature like a cheese until a cover was placed over it, is misplaced. Tellingly, the man who was retrospectively declared the founder of the Republic, Willem van Oranje, was born in what is now Germany, inherited the principality of Orange (France) and the title *Prins van Oranje*, received a French education at the court of Habsburg in Brussels (Belgium) and never intended to establish a republic.

In turn, the Republic unintentionally contributed much to the multi-faceted foundations of the modern Netherlands, even down to the current make-up of the population. The flourishing trade and the liberal climate attracted foreigners from far and wide, especially to Amsterdam which was growing at a rapid rate – from merchants and seamen to intellectuals and artists. By around 1620 almost three quarters of the population of the most important city in the province of Holland consisted of immigrants, especially those from the Southern Netherlands, reconquered by Spain.

More than three hundred years later, the Republic posthumously gave the Netherlands another multicultural impulse, when large numbers of migrants arrived from its former trade empire which transformed into a colonial empire during the nineteenth century. During the same period, the country started attracting migrant workers, particularly from Morocco and Turkey. The majority of these 'guest workers' intended to return home after a certain time, but in practice this rarely occurred and many actually brought their families over. The conspicuously ethnically and culturally diverse character of the current population was strengthened further by the admission of large numbers of refugees, especially during the final decade of the last century.

More than ten per cent of the Dutch population of nearly 16.4 million is of migrant origin. Most of these are non-western and live in the large cities. The largest migrant group of over 400,000 comes from the former colony of the Dutch East Indies. Once this country became independent under the name of Indonesia, large numbers of Dutch people living in the colony, persons of mixed Dutch-Asian heritage and Moluccans came to the Netherlands. When independence was proclaimed in the colony of Surinam, 145,000 Surinamese (a third of the population) migrated to the Netherlands. The Surinamese community of the Netherlands is now 344,000 strong. Over the years, 130,000 people made the journey from the Netherlands Antilles and Aruba – Caribbean islands which still form part of the Kingdom. The Turkish and Moroccan communities comprise 370,000 and 330,000 people respectively.

Ethnically, the Netherlands is not unlike the renowned Indonesian rice table: an extensive collection of dishes which still forms a whole. However, the integration of non-western immigrants has not always run as smoothly as was hoped. Particularly in the big cities, where on average one in three inhabitants is of foreign origin, it has led to some friction and unrest, which demonstrated above all else that not all indigenous Dutch people embodied the ideal of the tolerant and flexible cosmopolitan. Especially during economic dips, the reproach can be heard that the 'wilfully idle' come here to take advantage of the social provisions, which despite cuts are still among the most attractive in the world.

Immigration policy has been tightened in recent years, in view of the forecast that in forty years' time one in three Dutch citizens, nationwide, will be of foreign origin. Immigrants were also confronted with 'integration courses' intended to bring their knowledge of the language and society up to scratch. In early 2007, the Netherlands upheld its reputation as an innovative nation by becoming the first country to implement 'compulsory integration'. Non-western immigrants without Dutch nationality wishing to stay in the country long-term will have to sit an exam. They can expect questions on subjects such as arranging an electrical connection to a rental home, the way Dutch people greet each other and the name of the creator of a painting called *The Nightwatch*. All is explained to the prospective citizen in a comprehensive booklet. The text ends with: 'If you pass the exam, you have integrated. You will receive a diploma.'

This large-scale immigration has also had a great influence on the religious landscape. There are approximately one million Muslims in the Netherlands, and an estimated half of these visit a mosque regularly. In a short space of time, Islam has become the third organised religion after Catholicism and Protestantism, both of which have lost a great deal of ground in recent decades. Fifty years ago the Netherlands was one of the most god-fearing countries in Europe. It has since secularised at record speed. If you've ever dreamed of opening an office, bookshop or restaurant in a church building, or even living in one, the Netherlands is the place for you.

Nowadays, six out of ten Dutch people are nonpractising, but only a small proportion of these modern heathens call themselves nonbelievers. The rest believe that there is 'something', be it in heaven, between heaven and earth or hidden deep within the self. These are the adherents of what has been dubbed 'somethingism', now by far the largest religious movement, though it has barely involved any 'religious' organisation as yet. What connects the somethingists is, above all else, the need for meaning. Whether this is sought through like-minded people, tarot cards or a clair-voyant budgie is irrelevant to their labelling as a somethingist.

Despite the rise in secularism in recent decades, according to a view fashionable among Hollandologists, all Dutch people are in fact clergymen. This belief reduces every supposed Dutch trait to Calvinism, which became the preferred religion during the Revolt against the Catholic Spaniards. Commercial success, the love of the piggybank, the work ethic, the principle of equality and the sober lifestyle – it can all be traced back to John Calvin. However, it is evident that the support for the Calvinist churches, even in the days of the Republic, was too weak to serve as an all-embracing explanation of Dutch culture. Without wishing to disregard the influence of Protestantism, these days a greater emphasis is placed on the tolerant civil culture as the dominant heritage of the Republic.

The fact that this culture does not always function smoothly alongside the sharp edges of Protestantism is made clear in the

Dutch 'Bible Belt', which meanders with a dainty loop from the province of Zeeland via the Betuwe and the Veluwe up to the reed cutters reserve in Overijssel. This is where the hard core of the roughly 400,000 Dutch Reformed Church members live, who congregate in so-called 'black stocking' churches. Women's liberation is lost on these strict worshippers, and the renowned Dutch liberal legislation in areas such as abortion, prostitution, drugs and gay marriages is another thorn in their side.

These distinct viewpoints regularly lead to squabbles. No one is bothered by the community's practice of keeping the temptation of radio and television out of the home, but if a school refuses students because they have a television at home or read the 'wrong' version of the Bible, it can expect to be discussed in parliament. Also, the refusal on principle of around eleven thousand believers to insure or inoculate themselves is a recurrent political theme. It has been compulsory since the start of 2006 for all Dutch people to be insured for health costs but, in accordance with traditional Dutch practice, a legal exception was created for the 'scrupulous'.

The respected publisher of the authoritative Dutch dictionary, Van Dale, caused a great commotion with its intention to publish an expurgated version. This initiative was based on five Reformed Church schools in the 'black stocking' municipality of Staphorst. The 'Christian Van Dale' would differ from the existing dictionary on hundreds of points. For example, all references to genitalia and sexual activities were to be scrapped, including the words 'sex' and 'Viagra', as was anything with the remotest connection to swearing or any other vulgarity. The proposal found receptive ground with the League Against Blasphemy and Swearing, but everybody else accused Van Dale of selling its soul to the devil. Wisely, the publisher shelved the project.

Van Dale is the undisputed authority in the field of linguistics, and that bestows it a sacred status in the Netherlands, which has the greatest density of bookshops in the world. Language 'lives' in the Netherlands. It is not just that the Dutch read keenly and widely, or that the *Woordenboek der Nederlandse Taal* (Dictionary of the Dutch Language), at almost fifty-thousand pages, is the largest in the world; there is no other country where spelling revisions lead to so much turmoil.

This is certainly remarkable for such a small language. Dutch is spoken by around forty-five million people. Outside the Netherlands, this includes five million Belgians and the inhabitants of the former colonies of Surinam, the Netherlands Antilles and Aruba. Dutch is also spoken in a few European enclaves such as the extreme north-west of France, and then there is Afrikaans, spoken in South Africa and Namibia, an official daughter language of Dutch which the Dutch can reasonably comprehend. The knowledge of Dutch is fading in other countries with which the Netherlands has had intensive contact in the past, such as Indonesia. Even so, many Dutch words have found their way into foreign languages. The most notorious example of this is the word *apartheid*, understood without difficulty in large areas of the world.

The majority of foreigners who regularly visit the Netherlands or live there temporarily are unsuccessful in mastering the language. This double Dutch presents a number of major obstacles, especially the *ch* and *g* sounds. On top of that, those who persevere rarely get the opportunity to practise. If it's at all possible, the Dutch will address them in their own language. This helpfulness is regrettable, as it denies foreigners the opportunity to get to know a rich and dynamic language, which is also a source of amusement.

Follow the language and you will find the pulse of social development. *Scooter-Marokkanen* (scooter Moroccans) and other *hangjongeren* (youths who hang around) in *probleemwijken* (problem neighbourhoods), rejected *pardonkandidaten* (pardon entitlement candidates) who make use of the *uitzwaaiservice* (send-off service), *medelanders* (non-natives) who are deployed as *knuffelallochtoon* (cuddly migrant) and *excuusturk* (token Turk), animals which are *opgehokt* (caged up) or *preventief geruimd* (preventively culled) – it provides a fair idea of the problems the Dutch wrestle with, including their own taboos.

It becomes more amusing, and a sight more complicated, if, in addition to standard Dutch - *Algemeen Beschaafd Nederlands*, in short ABN – you also look into the several recognised regional languages and the enormous quantity of dialects which are often maintained with pride by their speakers. The high density of dialects is an unusual phenomenon which is often overlooked by compilers of lists of Dutch character traits. This demonstrates once again that the Netherlands is not culturally monotonous.

Although it is true that regional and local characteristics such as traditional costume, with the head brooches described in the past by many an amazed foreigner, only have any relevance in folklore now, regional pop music has undergone quite a revival: bands who sing in their own language are currently, to use proper Dutch, 'hot'.

Every Dutch person can sum up a couple of regions with their accompanying peculiarities. Just about everyone knows that life outside the *Randstad* is more agreeable than within it. To many, the most agreeable region is the 'Burgundian' Limburg, which is seen as the most un-Dutch part of the country, with its pretty hill landscape. 'It's like being abroad' is the standard comment of admiring Limburg-goers, who barely give the unique Dutch polder landscape a second look. The sing-song Limburgish with its soft *g* sound is a charming bonus, although this is also why the province is sometimes jokingly referred to as 'Limbabwe', a strange place with a strange dialect.

Without a doubt, the most obstinate Dutch people are to be found in the north. Not only are the Frisians known as stubborn and austere, they also speak a language that the average Dutchman cannot make head or tail of. Apart from ABN, Frisian is the only officially recognised language in the Netherlands. What the language means to the Frisians is demonstrated not only by the existence of a Frisian-Japanese dictionary, but also by the fact that since early 2007 the official name of the province is no longer the Dutch 'Friesland' but the Frisian *Fryslân*.

Within the still relatively young state of the Netherlands, there are many more regional and local idiosyncrasies, which in many cases are cherished. They are testimony to the individual historical developments that the districts of the biggest village in Europe have been through. The reed cutters and water farmers in the village of Nederland and the visible traces of the turf-digging in the De Weerribben National Park are examples of this.

This vast cultural, historical, ethnic and scenic diversity, bunched together in a small land area, is what makes the Netherlands what it is and is simultaneously its greatest peculiarity. Some characteristics are widely known, others are for connoisseurs. Some stick out like a sore thumb, while others require a certain in-depth knowledge that is lost on some people. The average Dutch person knows a thing or two about that. Mentioning the name of the prehistoric Funnelbeaker culture is more likely to remind him of a glass of Heineken rather than the megaliths of the province of Drenthe.

hEAD
aBOVE WAtER

Life at the bottom of the sea

In the beginning, was the sea. When that withdrew, man planted the potato on dried-out chunks of the earth's crust. As the brightest of all the species, he knew better than to do that on the water's edge. However, in one remote corner of the earth, a human species was evolving which was even more intelligent than the others. He quickly worked out that pushing the water even further back would be good for the potato crop. There might even be space left to do something with dairy products. Or bulbs.

Undaunted, he engaged in battle against the water. Just short of three thousand years later, the half-time score is 4-3 to Utopia-on-Sea, otherwise known as the Netherlands. The second half promises to be an exciting one. The rest of the planet has been shaking its head in bemusement for three thousand years.

But the longer the all-destroying flood that should have wiped out the Dutch experiment remained at bay, the greater the outside world's fascination became. On the quiet, the urge grew to go and take a look at exactly what those Dutch people were up to with their dikes, dams, barrages, bridges, locks and polders – a Dutch word that has now found its way into almost all of the world's languages. And, of course, to find out if they really did have webbed feet.

But one big question remained: is it safe there? Are there enough life buoys? After all, you never know. On arrival at Schiphol – the only airport in the world whose name is a reference to shipping – are you issued with a buoy by a scaly water nymph from the mighty Ministry of Water Management? 'Welcome to the Netherlands; here is your buoy. Although no storm flood has been forecast, we advise that you keep the buoy with you at all times. Yes, also on the bicycle. Enjoy your stay.'

It is astonishing how many foreigners view a trip to the Netherlands like a visit to a haunted house. It's exciting, but also a little bit creepy. Or, as in the case of my Indian friend, Kumar, terrifying and also a little bit exciting. In Kumar's village, sacred cows are the greatest threat to society. If you're unlucky, one might lumber into your house and eat your plants and tablecloth. Or you might crash head-on into one of these bulky creatures during a bike ride through the sandy streets. Kumar knows that this is nothing compared to the terrors suffered by the Dutch on a daily basis.

I reassure him, of course, but in honesty I was somewhat shaken myself when, around the age of ten, I was made party to the mystery at school. 'Boys and girls, a large part of the Netherlands is below sea level,' the teacher announced one sunny morning, which had passed normally until that moment. There had been no indication that lightning could strike at any time. Now that it had happened, the students sat and stared in bafflement. A jaw dropped here and there. No psychological aftercare was provided, and no one had heard of telephone helplines. We just sat there, dumbfounded.

I spent the rest of the day wondering desperately how such a thing could be: land below sea level. And of course, where this mysterious land could be found. I had seen the level of the sea before. You can see it from the beach, undulating away. I remembered it stank of fish. I had even touched it once, and tried, and sadly failed, to walk on it. I had looked underwater too, but all I could see was the sea bed. A dazzling sandy plain full of ripples. Strange, I thought, that the sand didn't dissolve in the salt water.

Still, I did understand that the bottom of the North Sea was the only possible location of the mysterious underwater land. There was a large pond not far from my home, but I'd never noticed any sign of life there, apart from the many, quacking ducks. I also thought this pond might be a little on the small side to accommodate a large portion of the population. No, it had to be the North Sea.

The rest of the riddle was child's play. Somewhere far from the coast, where the sea was deep enough, there was a huge, modern city. Blocks of flats stood in a row with, between them, dazzling four-lane roads, along which the population travelled in the ve-

hicle that was the Dutch contribution to the space age: the Daffodil 32, the marvellous Car of the Future with its *pientere pookje*
(smart gearstick) and Variomatic, a unique automatic transmis-
sion. The city was enclosed in a smooth glass bell jar. Like an
upside-down salad bowl, I explained to my friends, only bigger;
and guaranteed to be unbreakable.

Of course, my theory had a few flaws. For instance, how was
the bell jar connected to the mainland? Using submarines, I
reckoned. But then, how could they moor at the bell jar without
causing a deluge? And how did the city get its oxygen? Some
clever clogs had, no doubt, come up with a solution to all that.
A civilisation that had produced the Daffodil would know what
to do about such details. My theory was just as watertight as this
Dutch annex, I was certain.

I was all the more crestfallen when my teacher revealed the
shattering truth a week later. He used his pointer to draw a verti-
cal line across a map of the Netherlands. The area to the west of
this line was under water level, he explained cheerfully. About a
quarter of the country would be permanently underwater were it
not for sand dunes and river dikes. At high tide, three-quarters of
the country would be inundated. I felt myself sinking into a lake
of amazement. No glass city. No submarines. This underwater
land, we were right in the middle of it, school and all!

I remember looking outside involuntarily. The schoolyard
looked bone dry. A woman pushed a pram up the steep incline
of the street on which the school was built. I'd run up this street
as fast as I could if a dune gave way, I firmly resolved. Or I would
find out who had the key to the tower on the highest hill in town.
I wasn't quite sure whether that was a wise move, however: it was
a water tower.

This surprise at the alarming living conditions of the Dutch was ever thus. The Romans, at the beginning of our era, hit the mark when they classified the country as an inexplicably inhabited dwelling. To their dismay, they saw whole chunks of land floating off to sea, inhabitants and all. They probably meant the sparsely-populated peat bogs which covered the west and north of the country like vast cushions. Most of the population lived in the range of dunes along the coast and on the higher sandy and loamy ground of the east and south, where primitive dikes were supposed to offer protection against the river water. In the north, the Frisians had been building their villages on artificial hills up to fifteen metres high, called *terps* or mounds. This was the only way they could keep their heads above water. To Roman eyes, they were all castaways, the occupants of the delta of powerful rivers, created over the course of history by silt and sand deposits and bearing all the characteristics of an uninhabitable-declared dwelling.

It would take until well into the Middle Ages for the Dutch to finally shake off this image. They established the first major dikes around the year 1000. Shortly afterwards, the Frisians succeeded in drying out dike-ringed parcels of marshy territory. The first polders had been created, but there wasn't yet the technology for large-scale projects. This came in the fifteenth century in the form of the classic Dutch windmill.

This invention came not a moment too soon. In their zeal to exploit the boggy peatlands to the west, thus providing the growing urban population with fuel, the Hollanders brought a new problem on themselves. The exploitation artificially lowered the water level in the bog through the digging of ditches. And as bog is chiefly composed of water, this brought about the continuous subsidence of the ground which made the land behind the dunes increasingly vulnerable to flooding. Heavy storms regularly took their toll and centuries of bank erosion turned the dozens of lakes which had developed due to the peat excavation into an uncontrollable menace.

These perilous conditions formed a helpful stage for inventors and scholars whose names have gone down in history as hydraulic engineers. They were at the forefront of what had now taken on the character of a struggle against an enemy that had to be 'tamed'. Although their fame nowadays contrasts sharply with that of football prophets such as Johan Cruijff and Marco van Basten, the hydraulic engineers laid the foundations from which the modern Netherlands emerged. Some even launched plans to 'drive out the violence and poison of the North Sea for good' by encircling the entire country with a dam. This idea turned out to be somewhat ambitious. For the time being, they would have to content themselves with draining the many peat lakes using windmills which, connected in series, were capable of emptying vast pools of water.

A key role was reserved for a mill builder and hydraulic engineer with the exceptionally appropriate name of Jan Adriaanszoon Leeghwater ('Empty water'). He caused a furore in 1612 by draining the Beemstermeer lake to the north of Amsterdam using forty-three mills. The polder was laid out according to a strict geometric pattern. This orderly arrangement was to define the character of the Dutch landscape for centuries to come, and won the Beemster a place on UNESCO's World Heritage list in 1999. This list is now adorned by six 'items of Dutch cultural heritage', five of which are related to the battle against water.

Leeghwater poldered away happily, and also drew plans to drain the enormous Haarlemmermeer southwest of Amsterdam using two hundred mills. The immense peat lake, nicknamed 'the

Water Wolf', was expanding rapidly because of bank erosion and swallowing up whole villages. However, due to the high costs involved, but also the shipping and fishing interests of the towns of Haarlem and Leiden, Leeghwater's plan was put on ice. Only in the nineteenth century, once the occupants of Amsterdam and Haarlem had got their feet wet following heavy storms, was the Water Wolf taken by the scruff of the neck. After twelve years of unremitting labour the lake was drained in 1852. The Haarlem-mermeer was the first polder to be drained using steam-driven pumping stations, colossal machines which enabled the Dutch-man to perfect the art of impoldering. This polder is nowadays the location of the Schiphol national airport, five metres below sea level. The name ('Ship's hell') recalls the time when there was a treacherous bay here at low water, with the accompanying ship's graveyard.

The reclamation of the Haarlemmermeer put the Netherlands definitively on the map as a country of determined polderers and lock-keepers. The symbol of the eternal battle against the wa-ter was not the skilled engineers or the Haarlemmermeer itself, but a boy called Hans Brinker, from Spaarndam near Haarlem. Little Hans acquired worldwide fame after sticking his finger into a hole in a dike, thereby protecting the city of Haarlem from a disastrous flood. The American author, Mary Mapes Dodge, de-scribed the incident in 1865 in her international bestseller *Hans Brinker or The Silver Skates*. I was told this story at school during my youth. Just like the thriller about the mysterious underwater land, it made a devastating impression.

Of course, I wanted to poke a heroic finger into a leaking dike as well. Furthermore, if it would prevent the destruction of the fatherland I'd use two! I knew where to find a couple of dikes but there were no suitable holes to be found, which was in fact a relief as this meant the dikes weren't actually leaking. I'd keep a close eye on them, though. However, looking at the size of them, I started to cautiously doubt my intention to save the country. Would a little squirt like me actually be able to hold up such an awe-inspiring structure with one finger during a raging storm flood?

It became clear to me later on that the story about the brave Hans was made up. The author had never even been to the Netherlands. This did not stop her from assuring her young readers that her romantic description of the Netherlands as a land of mills, water, ice, skating and brave children was factual and that all Dutch people were familiar with the true-life adventures of Hans and his family.

Dodge described the Netherlands as a model state, whose inhabitants represented the pinnacle of creation and had elevated the plugging of dikes to an art: 'Not a leak can show itself anywhere, either in its politics, honor, or public safety, that a million fingers are not ready to stop it, at any cost.' Her book preceded a period of several decades around 1900 in which many Americans started to look upon the Netherlands as the true motherland of the United States, as the predecessor and source of inspiration of the 'American way of life'. The seeds of this were sown by the colonists who had founded New Netherland and whose capital of New Amsterdam would later become New York.

Interestingly enough, the book about Hans Brinker was nowhere near as successful in the Netherlands as in other countries. A full Dutch translation was only published over a hundred years after the original, which in the meantime had been turned into a film. Many Dutch people have heard of Hans and his heroic act but in general they are unaware of the finer details. For example, hardly anyone knows that the famous deed ascribed to Brinker is in fact the work of a different lad in the book – the anonymous 'Hero of Haarlem' – and that Hans has taken the credit undeservedly. Even so, this didn't stop the people of Spaarndam from erecting a statue in Hans' honour. They didn't have a great deal of choice when the first foreign tourists started to appear, enquiring about tangible mementoes of their hero, hardly known in the Netherlands. Statues of Hans Brinker were soon erected in Harlingen and the miniature city of Madurodam in The Hague as well.

During this period in which Dodge imagined her own Netherlands, writers who had actually visited the country also had work published. The 'wet' aspect was picked up by all of them. One claimed that the Netherlands was half water and only half land – and that wasn't even permanent, what with the frequent flooding. Another said that the entire country was anchored in the tumultuous North Sea. They were impressed by travelling by track boat through the waterways. Surprised travellers aboard the slow-moving barges noted that they could only see the roofs of the houses along the water front. The rest of them were hidden behind the dikes.

Opinions were divided on the occupants of these houses. The least complimentary were the French novelists Edmond and Jules de Goncourt, who in 1861 described the Dutchman as a type of amphibian: 'The men and women there are ugly, not in a human manner, but like fish, with fish eyes and fish heads, a complexion of dried fish, and they bear a resemblance to seals and frogs.'

Frogs or not, the visitors did agree on one thing: in order to prevent it from becoming a second Atlantis, the Dutch had transformed their country into a real bastion. This was expressed vividly by the Italian writer Edmondo de Amicis in 1874: 'The Netherlands is a fortress and the Dutch people live in it as if it is a fortress: on a war footing with the sea. An army of engineers, under the command of the Ministry of the Interior, keeps the enemy under constant supervision.'

The fortress so admired by De Amicis was to become considerably more robust during the next century. Several disastrous floods made it obvious to the Dutch that their bastion was far from watertight. In 1953, the southwest of the country with its many islands was, not for the first time, hit by a storm flood which claimed the lives of nearly two thousand people. The Dutch fought back with an unparalleled complex of dikes and dams which connected the islands, in doing so reducing the length of the North Sea coast from 1080 to 380 kilometres. The pinnacle of these Delta works is the storm flood barrier on the Nieuwe Waterweg, known as the 'eighth wonder of the world', completed in 1997.

Severe floods in the province of Noord-Holland in 1916 had already provided the impetus for the second grand enterprise: the Zuiderzee project, intended to tame the eponymous inland sea. The construction of the thirty-two-kilometre Afsluitdijk, a dam completed in 1932, downgraded the unpredictable Zuiderzee to an inland lake, known as the IJsselmeer. The largest polders in the world were then developed here: the Noordoostpolder (finished in 1942), Oostelijk Flevoland (1957) and Zuidelijk Flevoland (1968). Collectively they form Flevoland, the twelfth and youngest province of the country. The capital was christened Lelystad, a tribute to the brain behind the Zuiderzee project, the hydraulic engineer and Minister of Water Management, Cornelis Lely.

The three IJsselmeer polders are known as 'the new land'. And it still is new. The expansive green plains breath space, an effect that is intensified by the low clouds which are considered 'typically Dutch' thanks to the work of several famous seventeenth-century landscape artists. Perfectly straight roads, cycle paths and ditches, fringed by sharp lines of trees, reinforce the sense of space. During the summer, bright yellow blossoming rape sets the verges in flame. Large agricultural businesses set the scene. Spacious fields alternate with orchards, where signs advertise the house speciality: *'Appels van Dekker zijn extra lekker'* ('Apples from Dekker are extra delicious').

In accordance with Dutch tradition, the landscape has been laid out on the drawing table down to the square metre. The towns and villages are equidistant to each other and even the polder countryside has been meticulously designed. However, this does not make it any less abundant or impressive. Near to Zeewolde is the largest hardwood forest in Western Europe – planned, of course, down to the tree root. Also, the Oostvaardersplassen, a nature reserve between Almere and Lelystad, has spontaneously grown to become one of the continent's most important water-bird reserves.

Boring, interesting, fascinating – opinion on the artificial character of the landscape is varied. The fact is that enthusiasts come all the way from Japan and other distant places specially to see it. Another fact is that the landscape is slowly adapting to its users. The prefab buildings common on the industrial estates around the towns and especially the gigantic wind turbines which supply the farms with power are eyesores to many. In some places, forests of windmills have been developed which would panic Don Quixote.

The never-ending battle against water has made the Dutch world champions in water management. It is, in fact, an important and long-established export product. During the seventeenth century, Leeghwater journeyed to France and Germany to advise on major projects, and his colleagues advised and assisted the Venetian Republic. Even today, the city of the Doges is one of the many places where Dutch specialists work. In New Orleans, USA, Dutch companies are playing a significant part in repairing and reinforcing the dikes and flood barriers around the city which were hit hard by Hurricane Katrina in 2005. The Americans praise the 'Dutch approach' as the 'golden standard for storm risk reduction'. Elsewhere, too, there is profound respect for the work of the Dutch plumbers who, over the last millennium, have transformed their country from an inexplicably inhabited dwelling to a dry and comfortable place to be. The admiration reveals itself in the still famous words of the great French philosopher Descartes, who basked in the tolerant Dutch climate in the seventeenth century: 'God created the world, but the Dutch created the Netherlands.' That the Dutch had made a significant contribution to causing their country to be under water in those times with their peat excavation, is an aspect that is conveniently overlooked.

Is the Netherlands now 'finished'? It is anything but, and the Dutch are the first to recognise that there is not a single reason for them to rest on their laurels. That would be tempting fate in a country with the particularly appropriate name of the Netherlands – that lesson has been learned.

The fifty thousand kilometres of dikes and the thousands of big and small polders – altogether, sixty per cent of the territory – demand continuous maintenance and management. The latest technology is put to large-scale use in this, although the men of the Ministry of Water Management are equally happy to pull on the Wellingtons and get stuck in. There is also intensive experimentation with new, often spectacular methods of 'wetness management', like the laying of artificial reefs to protect the coast. And there are always new projects in the pipeline. For example, the Maasvlakte, a large industrial zone built in the North Sea which forms part of the port of Rotterdam, will in the near future have a sister even further out to sea.

Even so, vigilance is still advised, as demonstrated in the last fifteen years when on several occasions the wet enemy crept slyly up behind the Netherlands and overflowing rivers necessitated the evacuation of hundreds of thousands of people. A dike movement in 2003 fuelled doubt regarding the reliability of the dikes, designed to withstand the type of river flood which occurs on average once every 1250 years and to resist coastal high waters of a severity experienced only once every ten thousand years. Along with the steady rate of ground subsidence and the anticipated water level increase as a consequence of the greenhouse effect, this has led to new insights and measures. Riverbeds were deepened, dikes were even cut across and agricultural areas 'given back to nature' in order to create 'water overflow zones' – a form of 'depoldering' which pushed many Dutch people to the brink of an identity crisis.

The Thousand Years War, as they call the struggle against water in the province of Zeeland, will never come to an end, but hardly anyone in Utopia-on-Sea doubts its positive outcome. Yes, the sea giveth and the sea taketh away, as the graveyards in coastal areas attest, but the calling from the coast which turned the Dutch into fishermen, beachcombers, shipbuilders, traders and water managers has ultimately brought more advantages than disadvantages. Therefore, the tourist who on arrival at Schiphol asks for a life buoy is laughed at, or, for therapy, sent off on a bike to Nieuwerkerk aan den IJssel nearby Rotterdam. There, at 6.74 metres below sea level, is the lowest point in the Netherlands, and even Europe, and it's hardly any wetter there than at the highest point in the country – a 322-metre-high hill which, only in the flat, low-lying Netherlands, earns the title of 'mountain'.

GrEETINGS FROm
SODoM
aND GOmORRaH
Beacon of tolerance?

Life is pleasant in the *De Hollandse Leeuw* (The Dutch Lion) coffeeshop. Shrouded in palls of smoke and in various states of relaxation, the clientele enjoy a game and a chat around wicker tables. At the bar, the manager, a thickset man in his forties with a jolly face, passes the bilingual menu to a pair of British tourists. The menu displays about fifteen types of hashish and weed, alongside ready-rolled joints and home-baked 'spacecake'. Would the gentlemen require expert advice? 'Look, this is a nice weed, and that is too, and that's certainly a good weed. What? No, I don't know a damn thing about hash.' He walks over to the espresso machine, singing to himself; sure enough, they do actually serve coffee in the famous Dutch coffeeshops, after all.

These establishments, once described cautionarily by my best friend's grandmother as dens of iniquity where 'druggies inject hashish', are the international hallmark of the renowned Dutch tolerance. Wherever in the world the Dutch find themselves, sooner or later someone will ask if it's true what they hear about the coffeeshops. This is often followed by a second question: is it true that all Dutch people frolic naked on the beach, especially the women? The pinnacle of their astonishment is the fact that you can simply light up a joint on the street. The two Brits making a meal of rolling one in *De Hollandse Leeuw* spontaneously decide to enhance their jaunt through the land of freedom by asking a policeman for a light. That would be funny! The idea alone transports them to higher planes.

As well as being the breeding ground of water managers, the Netherlands is generally known internationally as a shining beacon of tolerance, freedom and permissiveness. This image is not founded solely on the liberal drugs policy. Equally celebrated is the open prostitution trade, which is regulated by law. The *Wallen* of Amsterdam are a world-class tourist attraction; for Dutch people, too. On any given summer's day, they can watch as hordes of foreigners file through the Red Light District, gawping at the scantily-clad ladies of pleasure who set out their wares in 'shop windows'.

Dutch law is known for being liberal and progressive in other fields too. For instance, the Netherlands was the first country in the world to legally recognise gay marriage. For decades, thousands of women every year have come here to have an abortion performed on them. Within the scope of 'human rights for women', one particular foundation even runs an 'abortion boat' which regularly moors off the waters of countries still in the era of the knitting needle – a service that is not equally welcomed by all countries. The law regarding euthanasia is also well-known to many foreigners. Some can even quote from the Constitution: 'Discrimination on the grounds of religion, personal convictions, political orientation, race, sex or any other grounds, is not permitted.'

'Live and let live': it is beyond dispute that this motto has been elevated to a fine art on the North Sea coast. The Dutch like to do their own thing, which they can, and they believe that everyone deserves a place in the sun. This point of view is also maintained emphatically for a broad range of the 'less well-off', such as the visually impaired, the disabled, young people, abused pets, homosexuals, the hearing impaired, lapsed Muslims, parents, hyper-intelligent toddlers, destitute seals, isolated 'burqa mothers', retired carrier pigeons, teenagers with learning difficulties, lonely donkeys – and, of course, hashish smokers. Each of these minority groups bask in the warmth of at least one pressure group which lobbies the government for special measures and provisions for the 'target group', and largely with success. It is often said in jest that the Netherlands has more action and pressure groups than inhabitants.

This same diversity typifies the political landscape. The firmly-anchored parliamentary democracy is populated nationally, provincially and locally by dozens of political parties. Under the Dutch voting system, it's not difficult to set up a new political party, and this does occur regularly. In 2006, the Party for Animals caused a shock by lodging itself in parliament with two seats. This is a unique phenomenon, but the party's energetic leader assures us this will not remain the case for long: 'The animal party phenomenon will spread around the world like an oil spill,' she predicts.

Unfortunately, not everyone recognises the land of sex, drugs and gay marriage as a paradise. What's more, to some it is downright appalling: 'A tolerant nation? Don't make me laugh! Totally indifferent, you mean!' According to these critics, the 'anything goes' mentality has turned the Netherlands into the plughole of civilisation. A ship without moral compass, heading straight for damnation, sails billowing. A modern-day Sodom and Gomorrah.

Even the famous Dutch cheese maid, the wholesome symbol of Dutch prosperity, regularly gets it in the neck. She has appeared on magazine covers with a joint in her mouth, a needle in her arm and in the guise of a cheese maid of easy virtue. The sharpest criticism in recent years came from the American media, which coldly referred to the euthanasia legislation as a way for the ever-pragmatic Dutch to do away with troublesome old folks. The country is up to its eyes in water, the devastating conclusion read, and it's only a matter of time before it goes under.

Funnily enough, the culture of mutual respect that many see as typically Dutch was actually developed in that water. Or, at least, in the battle against water. The necessity of keeping one's head above water taught the Dutch early on that consultation and cooperation were essential. The free peasants who, during the Middle Ages, settled in the peatlands in the west and north where the feudal system never took hold, were used to taking care of their own affairs. However, they realised that they would only be able to keep their place of settlement dry and habitable if they worked together. This need led to the development of the water boards. These, the oldest democratic administrative bodies in the Netherlands, would reach practical compromises regarding water management, once all those concerned had said their piece. The Dutch learned how to allow the diverse interests to be expressed as well as possible within the common interest: they became bridge builders in earnest, both literally and figuratively.

The consultation culture which originated in the polders developed into a general characteristic of administration and politics. Finding consensus became second nature to the Dutch. This explains why there always seem to be meetings taking place in Dutch offices, often lasting for hours, if not days on end, and preferably until late at night – otherwise, it seems, they do not count. According to a telling joke, any coincidental encounter between two Dutch people will turn into a meeting in no time at all. Just the sight of a large table with the ever-present thermos flasks of coffee unleashes the meeting-loving beast in every Dutchman.

At the end of the last century, the consultation culture created an international stir under the name of 'polder model'. The overseas admiration was aimed in particular at the regular consultation between government, unions and employers' organisations, intended to enable sensible economic development by means of give and take. An intensive form of polder model tourism was initiated among the international political elite, but economic stagnation soon turned the jubilation into criticism. The hallowed champions of the meeting were soon accused of being compromising, indecisive coffee freaks. References were even made to an older, much less flattering name for the consultation culture: 'the Dutch disease'. The polder model became the object of mockery. However, this did not dissuade the Dutch from continuing this deep-rooted tradition with zeal.

This is because the love of freedom and tolerance is in the genes of every Dutch person, concluded a German friend of mine after protracted research into the *Homo neerlandicus*. This profound insight had dawned on him when he was collared by a Dutch policeman after cycling through a red traffic light. To his dismay, the officer did not issue him with a ticket but instead pointed out amiably that his broken carrier strap was swinging dangerously close to his rear wheel. The policeman even wished him a pleasant day as he got back onto his third-hand bicycle. He realised that if even authority figures are tolerant, it must be genetic.

Conservative as I am, I will leave it as a cultural phenomenon for the time being, robustly anchored not only in the boggy medieval polder soil but also in the sixteenth-century Revolt of seven lowlands provinces against tyrannical Spanish rule. This rebellion was primarily a reaction to the Spanish persecution of Protestants, but took on the character of a war of independence over time, and culminated at the end of the century in the birth of the Republic of the Seven United Netherlands – a loose partnership of autonomous provinces which were compelled by circumstances to join forces. In a short space of time the little Republic grew into a superpower with a flourishing trading culture and an unprecedented degree of freedom and religious tolerance. For this reason it later became an inspiring example to other freedomloving rebels, in particular the American colonists who wished to rid themselves of British rule in the eighteenth century.

Freedom and tolerance were not absolute in the Republic. As a reaction to the Spanish persecution of the Calvinists, the latter were granted privileges and the Catholics were made to suffer. However, a blind eye was turned to their practising their faith within closed circles. This was the era of the Catholic conventicles, such as *Ons' Lieve Heer op Solder* (Our Lord in the Attic) in Amsterdam, which functions primarily as a museum nowadays.

Restrictions were also placed on other religions, but with time these became less oppressive. As long as 'dissidents' did not manifest themselves in public or hamper the government, they could do as they pleased. Even the privileged Calvinists were only able to interfere in political matters up to a certain extent.

The tolerant, civil and urban climate of the Republic held an enormous appeal for refugees and displaced persons who were persecuted in their own countries. At the end of the sixteenth century, many Portuguese Jews and even more Protestants from Antwerp and other cities of the Southern Netherlands found a safe haven there. These included a large number of merchants and intellectuals who made a significant contribution to the blossoming of what is called 'the first modern economy'. They were joined in the course of the seventeenth century by a large number of Jews from central and Eastern Europe and French Calvinists, known as Huguenots. The influx of foreigners – many of whom were employed on merchant ships and in the army – reinforced the international outlook that already characterised the Republic as a flourishing trading nation and brought society into contact with countless cultures.

The relatively great freedom of conscience and press made the Republic a free port for the soul. Following in the footsteps of the renowned Rotterdam humanist Desiderius Erasmus, intellectuals from home and abroad put their enlightened ideas down on paper and in cities such as Amsterdam, Deventer and Haarlem book production saw an unprecedented boom. During the seventeenth century, more books were published in the Republic than in the rest of the world put together. This included many works which were banned in other countries. 'Thus the first Amsterdam publisher to pass by, without being able to read, earned a million on a couple of Frenchmen who thought they could write,' noted the French philosopher Voltaire acerbically following a visit to the Republic.

However, there were limits, even for intellectuals. The Jewish philosopher Benedictus de Spinoza, prominent champion of freedom of conscience and tolerance, was posthumously banned from publication in the province of Holland due to his 'blasphemous, atheist views', which are now seen as some of the most important portents of eighteenth-century Enlightenment. It didn't stop the Hollanders from selling his work under the counter.

Interfering with affairs of state could also have unpleasant consequences, as the jurist Hugo de Groot found when he was sentenced to life imprisonment in Castle Loevestein for high treason. The fact that he was able to escape after two years – aptly enough, in a bookcase – was nothing less than historical justice for a man who is considered the founder of modern international law. However, he was compelled to write the books which earned him his great reputation in exile.

The tolerant climate of the Republic reflected the civic values of the powerful merchants, who also had a considerable stake in administrative affairs. Being practical and relatively broadminded, they saw the purpose of tolerance. Trade benefits from an atmosphere of freedom and mutual respect, and each customer is a customer, regardless of ethnic origin or political and religious conviction. As long as the necessary order was not disturbed, the merchants felt that each person should be allowed to do as he or she wished.

Moreover, their Calvinistic compassion for the disadvantaged brought about relatively modern provisions for orphans, the elderly, the poor and the sick. The institutions were popular attractions for foreign tourists. For a price they could even look around the prisons. In their opinion, the Republic was relatively humane:

torture, which was favoured elsewhere, was used only sparingly, and proportionally few villains ended their careers on the gallows. One of the reasons for this relative peace was probably that pickpockets and other petty criminals were thrown into the canal without mercy. As many were unable to swim, the Republic did not suffer from a shortage of prison cells.

A tolerant authority with an interest in the less well-off: my German friend would certainly have learned a thing or two in the Republic. Not discipline and tyranny but tolerance and diplomacy form the cement of a society in which the love of liberty goes hand-in-hand with the commonsense necessity of cooperation and sympathy for other opinions and cultures that is taken for granted. This doesn't mean everyone can cycle through red lights all the time, but that rules are sometimes applied flexibly. The traffic policeman must navigate a course between the indignation of the cyclist who is given a ticket and the same cyclist's call for law enforcement when the traffic gets hopelessly clogged up due to laid-back policing.

The restrained role of the government contributed to 'live and let live' taking on a unique form in the late nineteenth century. The still-sharp contrast between Protestants and Catholics – a popular maxim from the time was 'Two faiths on one pillow: the devil sleeps in between them' – and the deep rift between the religious and 'churchless' sections of the population, led to the society being split up as it were into socio-political segments or 'blocks', each with its own ideological character: Catholic, Protestant, social-democratic and liberal. These movements had their own political parties, unions, media, schools and hospitals, and as a result the lives of most Dutch people were played out entirely within their own environments. 'Everyone did his or her own thing', would be the way to describe it today. There was contact among the elites of the socio-political blocks. There, in the best tradition of the polder, intensive political debate took place to allow the segregated blocks to live together as peacefully as possible within the national state which was embraced by all.

In the first half of the twentieth century, there was unrest over this 'parochialism', but it would take until the nineteen-sixties for the system to collapse. In the Netherlands, the 'sixties had the same character in principle as elsewhere: everything had to change; it was time for action. Even the Dutch word for action (*actie*) had to change and it came to be written as *aksie*. It also gave an additional boost to the world of meetings, as any action had to be discussed democratically first. The Netherlands stood out because of the incredible speed at which these social changes took place and the negligible resistance put up by 'the establishment'. The churches were deserted at an alarming rate, bringing to an end the system of socio-political 'blocks'.

Another unusual characteristic was the 'playful' nature of many protests. The so-called *Provos* claimed a key role in publicity with playful provocation and 'anarchist action' such as using a smoke bomb to wreck the wedding of the current Queen Beatrix to her husband Prince Claus, who died in 2002. Also, the 'feminist action group' *Dolle Mina* (Mad Mina), which demanded legalised abortion under a slogan which translates as 'boss of one's own belly', shocked the nation by displaying naked navels. Youngsters from all over the world headed *en masse* for Amsterdam to realise their dreams, thousands spending the night at Dam square and in Vondelpark – named after the Netherlands' most famous poet of the seventeenth century, who was himself not averse to poetic protest against the authorities.

In the wake of this social upheaval, the Netherlands took on the character traits which made it the world champion of tolerance in the eyes of many: the great personal freedom and the liberal legislation which assures the existence of the abortion boat and the *De Hollandse Leeuw* coffeeshop. Furthermore, the polder model survived the barricades intact. The Dutch still swear by co-operation and debate, and this has been increasingly necessary in recent years. The word 'tolerance' is the main topic on the current agenda. The reason for subjecting the cherished term to further inspection was formed by two political murders which sent the country headlong into a state of confusion.

A good week before the Lower House elections of 2002, the flamboyant but controversial scientist-politician Pim Fortuyn was shot dead by an environmental activist. According to opinion polls, Fortuyn and his hastily-assembled party stood a decent chance in the elections, and he had his own eye on the position of prime minister. The party did indeed cause a political upheaval but soon disintegrated due to amateurism and internal squabbles.

The murder shook the country to its foundations, as did the 'Fortuyn revolt'. How was it possible that someone had come from nowhere to acquire such large support, and without any electoral platform worth mentioning? How come it was, of all people, a vain dandy with two white lap dogs, who paraded his homosexuality and visits to 'dark rooms', who was embraced by the 'common people' as 'our Pim'?

Fortuyn attributed his success to the fact that he drew attention to problems and discontent which for a long time had passed politicians and media by. That applied in particular to the problems concerning the integration of part of the Islamic population – in the wake of September 11th 2001, a more topical subject than ever.

Fortuyn homed in on the feelings of many residents of the older urban districts in which these problems were most keenly felt. He also sharply criticised what he called the 'arrogance and shortcomings' of the 'left-wing church': the 'self-satisfied, so-called progressive political elite', which had drifted miles from reality with its high ideals of integration and had nothing left to offer voters in working-class areas. Fortuyn promised to 'give the country back to the people'.

Fortuyn found not only support but resistance. It was true that he had shown the nation a collective blind spot, but he made himself widely unpopular with his theatrical performances, provocation and straight-talking statements, such as 'Islam is a backward culture'. His motto was 'I say what I think and I do what I say'. However, many Dutch people found as little to identify with in the song and dance he created as 'the people' did in the views of the 'left-wing church'.

While the shock of Fortuyn's murder was still reverberating and the Dutch comforted themselves with the knowledge that, at least, the killer was not an immigrant or a Muslim, a second blow was struck in 2004: the columnist and film-maker Theo van Gogh was brutally murdered by a radical Muslim. For years, Van Gogh had turned insulting people into a fine art. He provoked everyone imaginable and made himself almost impossible to employ as a columnist. He invariably referred to Muslims as 'goatfuckers'. Many Dutch people loathed him for this but his violent death was seen unanimously as an assault on tolerance.

Since then, the 'I say what I think' virus has spread, and Muslims are often the target. The most prominent of these voices is the politician Geert Wilders, who frequently makes the front pages with provocative statements about 'backward' Islam, the threat of a 'tsunami of Islamisation' and the 'fascistic' Koran, which he feels should be banned. Many Dutch people accuse him of boorishness and sowing fear and hatred, but he is seen particularly by former supporters of Fortuyn as a figurehead in the struggle against a handful of imams and their orthodox beliefs. His mission is being met with a series of death threats, and Wilders has been under permanent protection for several years.

The Dutch stare at each other in bewilderment. What have we done to deserve this polarisation of social relationships and the traditionally thoughtful, sometimes even evasive debate, they wonder. What happened to mutual respect? And more pertinently, how tolerant are we really? Have we, after all, fallen prey to an 'anything goes' mentality?

It can do no harm to consult foreign experts, who are able to survey the battlefield from a distance, in the search for answers. Don't worry too much, is often their advice to the Dutch. Your open society can take a knock, that much is clear. And, as far as your tolerance goes: in other countries two political murders would have led to a massive eruption of violence. There have been no violent repercussions in the Netherlands.

This doesn't stop many Dutch people from feeling uneasy, all the more because this tolerance seems to be displaying yet more cracks. For example, 'queer-bashing' seems to have made an unpleasant comeback recently. Even in Amsterdam, would you believe, which still proudly asserts itself as the gay capital of Europe, homosexuals are feeling increasingly unsafe. It's an odd phenomenon: while all the research seems to point to an ever increasing acceptance of homosexuals, a small number of homophobes are seeking refuge in violence. The police force is considering using 'decoy homosexuals' to entrap queer-bashers, though the method is a controversial one. Similar experiments with 'decoy prostitutes' and 'decoy bikes' led to discussions regarding the legal soundness of this approach.

And, as if the classic tolerance has not had enough to endure, the government intends to tighten the notorious 'policy of tolerance' towards soft drugs, the hallmark of Dutch permissiveness. 'Tolerance' it indeed is, as despite what most foreigners think the use of soft drugs is not permitted by law. It is only 'tolerated' as long as it does not cause too much trouble. In that respect, the coffeeshops are similar to the seventeenth-century Catholic conventicles. Local authorities have a large say in this policy and in some smaller towns it's not a good idea to ask a policeman for a light for your joint, although the days when you would have been thrown into the canal for it are long gone.

To the predictable dismay of many a tourist, it looks as if the number of coffeeshops will decline in the near future. Initially, to discourage the use of cannabis among young people, they must disappear from the vicinities of secondary schools. Dope-smoking will also be made less appealing in certain border municipalities. It has long bothered authorities in some neighbouring countries that their subjects seem to enjoy themselves so much in the Dutch 'narco-state'. Evidently, the fact that their own drug problems are often greater than those of the Netherlands, despite stricter laws, is deemed irrelevant.

Although he himself has nothing to fear from such measures, the manager of *De Hollandse Leeuw* has reservations about this gnawing away of Dutch tolerance: 'They should all keep their hands off it. Yes, off the gays and the Muslims too.' Fortunately, he's always ready with expert advice: 'That Wilders fellow should come round here for a nice smoke. And he should bring the prime minister and that bunch of queer-bashers with him.'

aBNoRMALLY
NORMAL

A sea of idiosyncrasies

The Dutch are, on average, the tallest people in the world. They tower sky-high over their flat landscape, and when travelling in countries populated by shorter people they need to duck to avoid continuously hitting their heads against doorposts and luggage racks on public transport. The average Dutchman measures 1.81 metres from head to toe, and the average woman 1.68. Another 4.5 centimetres is added on top of that in each new generation. If this goes on, the taller of the two, who every weekend proves himself a fanatical do-it-yourself enthusiast, can expect to have a serious job on his hands in a few generations' time.

It's an amusing and fascinating fact, this world record. How is it that the tallest people have arisen from the insignificant polders? If you live a few metres below sea level, do you grow that little bit more quickly towards the sunlight? It's more likely that we will find the answer in Dutch cooking. The robust mashed dishes and dearly beloved potatoes and dairy products in the Dutch pantry are often branded as glorified dog food by foreign gourmets, but they can't be that bad after all. The additional fact that the Dutch are also among the healthiest people in the world indicates that there must be at least something good going on in their kitchens.

In many countries, such facts are seen as unusual, even heartening achievements, and that is only human. Not something you'd display immediately in a trophy case like a flashy cup, but you'd give it a place on the mantelpiece. In the Netherlands, however, this world record barely registers. Unusual? How come? What do you mean; it's quite normal isn't it? At worst, it's a bit sad for those who aren't all that tall and healthy. Aren't they entitled to bang their heads against luggage racks? Shouldn't we see if we can do something about that? After all, we're all equal, aren't we?

It's an unusual trait, this tendency of not seeing one's own peculiarities as peculiar at all. *Gewoon zijn* (being normal) is one of the highest virtues one can possess in the Netherlands, and emphasising peculiarities does not fit in with that at all. Most Dutch people are not at all interested in anything that smacks of such national 'grandeur'. That their society, including its remarkable tendency towards 'normality', is in every respect the product of a rich past, is something they are barely conscious of. The typical answer to the question of why they are the way they are is

'Nou, gewoon!' ('Well, we just are!'). Were the roots of enterprise, modesty and simplicity already in the soil of their once-uninhabitable swampy delta with its long coastline? I expect so. Was the seventeenth-century Republic of the Seven United Netherlands the 'first modern economy' and for decades, the economic, political and cultural centre of western civilisation? Eh? Republic? What republic? And did the civil, urban Dutch culture of the era give rise to the modern ideals of freedom and equality? Surely not! Really?

Let's not pretend to be bigger than we are, is the Dutchman's motto. When visitors tell him that his country is homely, prosperous and progressive, he doesn't mind, but not without adding that at the same time it is too small to really matter much. It's not without reason that he is full of diminutives – even the word *gewoon* has a miniature version: *gewoontjes*. Many foreigners express surprise at the minuscule teaspoons and the ever-so-cosy but, by western standards, often cramped homes. We are all equal, say the Dutch, and that's how it should be, otherwise it wouldn't be fair, and we can't have things being unfair, there's no defending it, it's simply not acceptable. It's as simple as that.

Of course, even in the Netherlands, not everyone is equal. Even if it's just because some are taller, or more talented, than others. However, the Dutch have an elegant solution to this little fault in creation: if, heaven forbid, we are not all equal, at least we all have the right to be equal.

'Equal opportunities for all' is an ideal that is in the genes of the Dutch. And, one has to say, they have gone a long way towards achieving it. All Dutch people enjoy the spoils of one of the most highly-developed welfare states in the world. In addition, there is a maze of schemes and safety nets aimed at giving those who are 'less well-off', 'miss the connection' or are 'in danger of slipping through the net' opportunities to better themselves socially. These provisions are an example to us all, in the views of many foreigners, but the Dutch think it's all very normal. Typically, critical debates always revolve around 'a little bit more' or 'a little bit less' but never around the abolition of the system.

This penchant for equality is rooted in the struggle against water, and gained an enormous boost from the Enlightenment of the eighteenth century: the equality of all citizens was established in the first Constitution of 1798. A new offensive followed in the nineteen-sixties and 'seventies: everybody who was in a 'disadvantaged' position had to be able to 'take part'. Up to the present day, this noble urge is visible in all shapes and forms, from job application courses for the long-term unemployed to language and sports courses for immigrants. Some local authorities organise cycling courses to get Islamic women out of social isolation. And in the province of Drenthe, visitors to the 'People Library' were able to have a chat with 'loan people' around whom there may exist prejudices or misunderstandings, such as politicians, civil servants and foreigners. Simultaneously, over the course of time whole sections of the population have been freed from 'stigmatising' labels. The disabled, for instance, are now known as 'people with possibilities'.

The drive for emancipation is not restricted to social and cultural areas, but also conquers biological limits. Children whose growth is in danger of 'falling behind' are sometimes given medicines to stimulate growth. Little wonder that the Dutch are the tallest people in the world, shorter nationalities mutter – we would be, in their position, too.

The machinery that is supposed to forge Dutch society into an orderly whole of equal, satisfied and rational citizens is incredibly complex. The busybodying displayed by the Dutch in draining and setting up their country is nothing compared to the apparatus behind the Welfare & Happiness department. The task of the tens of thousands of W & H staff is not a thankful one. In the consultation meetings which precede every new measure, they are faced with a cacophony of wishes. They have to prevent the requirements of one from being fulfilled at the cost of those of another. Moreover, citizens turn up at the counter uninvited, loudly demanding their rights, such as the right to additional childcare for new parents who perceive a threat to their busy careers, social obligations and two cars – in a nutshell, their right to develop themselves.

Then again, there are many Dutch people who feel that it is the bureaucracy that is an obstacle to their welfare and happiness. A businessman who created Europe's largest wild-water rapids in Zoetermeer was required to possess twenty-three permits to do so, involving the commission of 135 studies. It cost him two million euros. 'In this country, everyone is keeping everyone else busy,' he grumbled. He's not the only one. The promise to hack through the jungle of laws, procedures and regulations is an evergreen among election pledges. The trouble is that this often demands new bureaucratic measures in turn.

Despite all the bumps and potholes, the Netherlands is in many respects not only literally but also figuratively the most egalitarian country in the world. The disparity of incomes is relatively small. An eternal bone of contention is represented by the hefty salaries, bonuses and golden handshakes which are common at the highest echelons of industry. In relation to this the former Prime Minister, Wim Kok, referred to 'exhibitionistic self-enrichment', which touched a few nerves. Ten years later, the cry still echoes through the land, accompanied by the clamorous call for the implementation of a 'grab tax'. The average Dutchman gives not a hoot for the argument that top managers will head for foreign climes if they do not receive a comparable income in the Netherlands. It's high time they started dealing with this madness over there too, says he. Because, let's be frank: why is one of these directors worth more than I am? Well, there you are.

A trait of this equality that seems remarkable in foreign eyes is the Dutch habit of starting to use each other's first names at the soonest opportunity. Managers whose staff bluntly refer to them by their first names and sometimes receive a hearty slap on the shoulder – it's not easy for foreigners to get used to. The informal business culture has other exotic facets which cause brows to furrow. Employees who turn up at the office in leisure wear – even shorts – and employers who walk into staff meetings without a tie would in many countries be shipped off to reserves for endangered species. And, in such cultures, a manager who answers the phone with a melodious '*Met Piet*' ('Piet here') could look forward to a career in charge of the Paper Recycling division.

To the amazement of many foreigners, this levelling-out also has the education system in a stranglehold. Who would teach infants to address their teachers by their first names? Or, stranger still, to prefix that name with a prehistoric title such as 'master' or 'miss'? And don't those children get confused by all these Master Jans and Miss Marias, the most common first names? And why do the Dutch refuse to select students for university education? What's wrong with elite universities? Why should everyone be able to join in? Shouldn't you develop talent and reward those who are outstanding?

This criticism of university training strikes at the heart of the Dutch culture of equality. Elevating the 'disadvantaged' is what that is all about. The elite can take care of itself, is the idea. High-flyers are not celebrated in the Netherlands unless they demonstrate that they have actually 'remained normal'. There's nothing better than the working-class boy who makes it but nevertheless remains 'himself'. However anyone suspected of having airs and graces will not get very far in the popularity polls.

This is what happens to, among others, the well-off people who flaunt their wealth. Whereas previous generations were still characterised by modesty, the younger generation is much more likely to show off, for example in the latest 'sport utility vehicles', flashy beasts of vehicles which are known in the vernacular as *patserbakken* (yup mobiles) and – after the most chic shopping street in Amsterdam – *P.C. Hooft tractors*. Their lot is tar, feathers and an old Dutch saying: *'Doe maar gewoon, dan doe je al gek genoeg'* ('Just be yourself – that's strange enough').

The egalitarian Dutch do not hold much truck with heroes either. This was the experience of seventeenth-century naval heroes like Piet Heyn, Maarten Harpertszoon Tromp and Michiel de Ruyter, long celebrated because of their great contributions to the nation's glory during the Golden Age. In addition, they were true working-class boys whose ambitious exploits were avidly followed and loudly applauded by the masses: Heyn's capture of the Spanish silver fleet in 1628, Tromp's victory over a large Spanish war fleet in 1639 and De Ruyter's attack on the English war fleet in 1667.

However, during the latter half of the twentieth century, these heroes posthumously fell overboard. On further inspection, wasn't a chap like De Ruyter a ruthless soldier who also defended Dutch interests in the slave trade? And in all our refinement, hadn't we got used in the meantime to talking out our conflicts rather than fighting them out? Their lot was shared by Joannes van Heutsz, who, circa 1900, led the bloody 'pacification' of Aceh in the Dutch East Indies, the only region in which the Netherlands flexed its military muscle during the nineteenth and twentieth centuries. He received a hero's welcome on his return to the fatherland, but was retrospectively pushed aside as an imperialist villain.

Uncomfortably feeling their way, the Dutch have recently tried to regain contact with their exiled heroes. The Netherlands hesitantly commemorated the four-hundredth birthday of Michiel de Ruyter in 2007. But new heroes are rigorously screened. In recent years there have been statues of Pim Fortuyn, the murdered politician, and André Hazes, the deceased folk singer, both of whom were wildly popular. The message is clear: if you're not a working-class hero, no statue.

It's a good thing, and at the same time a characteristic feature, that there is barely a visible sign of any nobility in the Netherlands. The lords and ladies would be nailed to the pillory at the first sign of ostentation. There is of course a royal family, but that's as 'normal' as a royal family can be. Eighteenth-century foreign visitors were already astounded by the Oranjes: they would simply walk the streets with their servants in tow, even at the fair.

The current queen, Beatrix, is an unusually 'normal' queen and that's how she appears too, without the usual pomp and splendour associated with monarchs. Her only distinguishing mark is her always eye-catching hat, but even that is no longer an exclusively royal privilege. On *Prinsjesdag*, when the queen solemnly announces the government's intended policies for the new parliamentary year in the Queen's Speech, all of the women present wear headgear which is either eye-catching, odd, silly or downright absurd. Members of Parliament whose most daring item of clothing is usually a pearl necklace suddenly surge along like battleships with billowing sails. The media are right on the scene.

Of course, the queen does have a royal household, with real lackeys, and she lives in a palace. But that's fine, otherwise she wouldn't be a real queen. However, her palace is a modest one, and in other monarchies it wouldn't amount to much more than a coach house. This modesty is characteristic of all Dutch architecture: apart from a few exceptions, the cities lack pompous monuments and grandiose squares and avenues where one might hold a good old parade. Like the rest of society, the street scene breathes the atmosphere of an out-and-out civil culture.

That's also how the Dutch prefer to see their politicians: as 'normal' citizens who seem to be connected with 'the people'. Ex-prime minister Wim Kok detested official lunches at the time; he preferred to eat his homemade cheese sandwich at his desk, washed down with a glass of buttermilk. That's the kind of prime minister they like in the Netherlands. Similarly, a minister who cycles to work cannot put a foot wrong.

Internationally, the frugality of the Dutch is not always valued. During the 1997 European summit in Amsterdam, the Dutch host nation treated all the European heads of government to a bicycle. Not everyone appreciated the frivolous gesture. Even grander was the gesture by the Minister of Defence, who in early 2007 received a high Afghan distinction in Kabul as a token of gratitude for the Dutch military effort in Afghanistan. The Dutch minister surprised the Afghan president with the gift of a pair of clogs.

It's no coincidence that the Dutchman is known worldwide as an incorrigible skinflint, whose favourite animal is the piggy bank. One of the stubbornest clichés doing the rounds is that he will serve one, and only one biscuit with a cup of coffee. The English language contains unflattering expressions like 'going Dutch' and 'Dutch treat', in relation to the custom of sharing the bill after a pleasant meal out. And if you mention that you are from the Netherlands at a market in Egypt, the traders will howl in chorus *'Kijken, kijken, niet kopen!'* ('Looking, looking, not buying!'). It's the only Dutch they know.

The Dutch have had the reputation of born penny pinchers for centuries. In earlier times, they were even considered by some to be downright swindlers, who had no qualms about selling their souls to the devil. If there was money to be made, they were happy to trade with the enemy, transport tens of thousands of slaves from Africa to the New World, or nonchalantly throw their bibles overboard – according to one persistent rumour, this was done in return for the right to be the only European nation allowed to trade with Japan for over two centuries from 1636 on. The entrepreneurs adopted the Calvinist principles of industry and austerity, which went merrily hand-in-hand with the merchant trade. You can still see the maxim *'De cost gaat voor de baet uit'* ('Nothing ventured, nothing gained') on Golden Age facades. However, when it came down to it, the merchant triumphed over the equally-dominant clergymen. 'Land of canals, ducks, scoundrels,' the eighteenth-century French philosopher Voltaire called the proud Republic of the Seven United Netherlands. The 'scoundrels' were the swindlers who cheated him out of money.

So, a nation of born penny-pinchers: the Dutch are still saddled with that image. There is plenty of evidence: the myth of that one miserable biscuit of course, but also popular domestic tools like the bottle-scraper, the 'Vacu Vin' and the cheese slicer, symbol of nauseating thriftiness.

Certainly, the Dutch have been thrifty since way back when. But to most people, this frugality wasn't so much a hobby that had got out of hand as a dire necessity. If you didn't save for 'later on' – in the proverbial old sock beneath the mattress – you might end up with a nasty surprise. This sentiment has lodged deep in the soul, because even when things slowly started to get better for him, the Dutchman carried on saving frantically. In no other country is insurance so popular. The Dutch like to keep the upper hand over destiny and as such are world champions in saving and insurance by some distance.

The winged expression *'Wie wat bewaart, die heeft wat'* ('Waste not, want not') is also reflected in the Dutchman's attic. Since time immemorial, things that are no longer used but are still usable have been kept, sometimes for generations. Who knows, they may come in handy one day. You can always still throw it away, although to many Dutch people that is still *zonde* (a waste).

Companies like Unilever and Albert Heijn cleverly take advantage of this. For years, Albert Heijn's supermarkets have done excellent business during the 'Hamster Weeks'. No consumer is insulted by the comparison with a rodent that stocks up so dauntlessly. Quite the opposite is true: many a Dutch person honours the title set aside for him by filling the pantry to the rafters during the Hamster Weeks.

The slogan *'Geen cent teveel!'* ('Not a cent too many!') chirped by a good-humoured farm girl used by the Dutch-British multinational Unilever to praise its *Zeeuws Meisje* (Zeeland Girl) margarine brand, was an instant hit. The popularity of the brand was abundantly demonstrated when the company debated removing it from the market. The consumer was not happy, and Unilever gave the lass from Zeeland a second chance.

A second Dutch-British multinational, fuel supplier Shell, had a much harder time when it resolved to cease to issue its popular savings stamps. Shell saw it as an old-fashioned customer relations exercise, but the consumer thought differently. The consequences were a national outcry and a threat to boycott Shell stations. In the view of the Dutch, collecting stamps was an 'acquired right'.

Even so, the urge to save seems to be on the wane. It's true that the Dutch still save more than any other prosperous nation, but the younger generations who have grown up in affluence, are happy to spend more freely than their parents and grandparents. What about the perceived thrift of the Dutch, then? The figures shatter this image, and in fact point out the opposite. The Dutch are the first to open their wallets when there are collections for victims of disasters and those in need, and regularly top the international donor league. Other good causes are also given to generously. And, by international standards, the Netherlands has a very large army of volunteers who roll up their sleeves for their numerous clubs and a wide variety of charities. In reality, the Dutchman has never been a tightwad – no more than the cheese slicer is a Dutch invention. That honour is reserved for a furniture maker from Lillehammer in Norway.

The restrained gifts with which Dutch officials expect to impress their foreign colleagues are not the only legacy of the past. The Dutchman's strong international orientation is also down to this. Dutch merchants have long been crossing borders to trade. And because of these trade interests, Dutch politicians have for centuries promoted peace, international cooperation, free trade and international rule of law. It's no coincidence that the Netherlands was one of the founders of the European Union and is proportionally one of the largest donors to the United Nations, in addition to being the location of the International Court of Justice and the International Criminal Court. To a certain extent, the Dutch voting against the European Constitution in a referendum in 2006 was a historical absurdity. This chorus of disapproval reflected fears for a European 'superstate', but was mainly a 'no' towards a disgraceful government campaign which held out the prospect of hell and damnation to the citizen were he not to vote 'yes'.

Internationally, the Dutchman is known as open, interested, flexible, punctual, good with languages, and down-to-earth – a cool customer, even, in reference to his climate. He is also known as being a straight talker who 'calls a spade a spade'. Circumspection often wins the day in international business and politics, but the Dutchman 'steers a straight course' like a clog-wearing bull in a china shop. He would rather give his unadulterated opinion than allow potential misunderstandings to exist, even if it is only to 'make things discussible'. Not everyone views this trait as a virtue. In some cultures, being straightforward is seen as tactless or even rude and abrupt – and a bull in a china shop is a clumsy oaf, albeit a well-meaning one.

The Dutch are also sometimes misunderstood and criticised when disseminating their ideals. Convinced of the universal legitimacy of their own views they tend to want to persuade the whole world of the benefits of equality, freedom, liberation, development work and the right to bang one's head on luggage racks in buses and trains – all these things are absolutely 'normal' and everyone is entitled to them. The 'abortion boat' is part of a rich Dutch tradition. However, in its role of 'model country' the Netherlands is regularly reproached for being a meddlesome and pedantic preacher.

Take a look at yourselves first, say the critics. Or are there no problems anymore in the polders? What about the discrimination against foreigners and women? And where do those queer-bashers come from? And why does your candour turn to reticence and inept stammering when it comes to your own scandals?

The sense of injustice that bubbles up within the Dutchman when reproached in this fashion demonstrates that he is anything but the cool customer he is held to be. A single visit to a football match will rid you of that misapprehension. And the misapprehension on which that one is based, too: it doesn't really rain 366 days a year in the Netherlands. Not by a long shot, in fact. Actually, the climate is quite varied, and each of the four seasons has a charm of its own. The Low Countries have something for cool customers and hot-blooded sun-worshippers alike.

Nonetheless, the rain is one of a select range of topics on which the Dutch like a heartfelt moan from time to time. Other prominent butts of national grumbling include the Dutch Railways, bureaucracy, Hague politics, Islam, spelling reforms, and, public enemy number one, the alleged injustice concerning the distribution of income, such as the abuse of welfare provisions and the 'grabbing culture' in industry. For the equality-loving Dutch, this theme will most likely be a source of inspiration until the end of time. As long as no one is asked to divulge their own salary. They would rather confide their private sexual deviances in those around them than their financial situations.

Foreigners who have to listen to all that moaning could easily get the impression that the Netherlands is a vale of tears. That couldn't be further from the truth. Again and again, research shows that the Dutch are one of the happiest populations in Europe. Dutch teenagers are even the happiest in the world.

Research reveals that the unhappiest Dutch people live in The Hague. Everyone can understand why that is so. With the government and parliament just around the corner, despondency is guaranteed, goes the national wisdom – a thousand W & H workers won't change that.

On the other hand, no one understands why the happiest Dutch people live in the province of Overijssel. Happy in Ommen? Come on. You wouldn't want to be seen dead there. Could it have anything to do with the Bible Belt that stretches over part of the province? If so, the research doesn't mean anything. The inhabitants of that world would be happy anywhere; they see any domicile as the vestibule of heaven.

Perhaps that is where you will find the answer to the question of why the Dutch are so happy: despite all their moaning and their unremitting efforts to improve their own society and, by extension, the rest of the world, they regard their paradise of equality as heaven on earth. Although, it seems, that is so 'normal' that they barely notice it.

5 GoING
PLAcES

A land of sights to see

On average, foreigners visiting the Netherlands stay for around three days. With all due respect to full diaries, limited budgets and the temptations of other destinations: that's not the way to do it. When the Dutch go abroad, at least they are polite enough to stay for a week. Even if their destination is a gross disappointment, they are robbed twice and after one day develop a heartrending homesickness for floury potatoes. What is more important is that the Netherlands is a terrific holiday destination:

incredibly versatile and blessed with a tenacious, friendly population and excellent facilities. Apart from a serious case of the Dutch disease – the notorious phobia of expansive, flat spaces – there is no excuse whatsoever, once you've got over the dikes, for not spending an entire holiday in the Netherlands.

Let's assume you haven't come here for the amusement parks, though there are many, but you're mad about historical towns. If so, you're in trouble, as there are dozens of them. You won't scratch the surface in three days. Don't even try. Do you want to alternate enjoying canals, bridges and facades with museum visits? You're absolutely right to, but there's a problem: even if the museums were open twenty-four hours a day, you could forget covering them in three days. You're in the country with just about the highest density of museums in the world. You'll notice that yourself, anyway.

Perhaps you're a nature lover, and want to get stuck into the country's flora and fauna? That shouldn't be a problem, you think, in such a small country which insiders have assured you is as flat as a pancake. The last thing I want to do is spoil the anticipation for you, but to start with we've got a handful of Frisian Islands each of which are worth a couple of days' exploration. On top of that there are about four hundred highly varied nature reserves full of remarkable plants and animals.

If you are a nature fan, you could of course start with the beaches. The Netherlands has a broad, white rim which is more impressive than most foreigners are prepared to believe, and you can gain a fair experience of it in three days. With major climate change on the way, the beaches have a golden future in tourism. In a few centuries' time, palm trees will be growing on them. The trick will be to protect them against rising sea levels, but then the Dutch are good at that.

Until then, you can choose on a sunny summer's day between the crammed beaches of Zandvoort and Scheveningen and quieter places elsewhere on the coast. Even when there's no sun the coast is a great place to visit. There's nothing as refreshing as taking in the air on the beach and in the dunes. Therefore, it's not a bad idea to start your holiday in the Netherlands with a good beach walk, so that you can weigh up the enormous array of attractions, consider them fully and make a choice: to get things straight between your ears, so to speak. That's just what the Dutch do when they walk on the beach. It's due to this popular phenomenon that Dutch healthcare is still at all affordable.

What else can you do in the Netherlands? Or rather, what can't you do? A list was recently presented, to some fanfare, of seven new wonders of the world. The compilers could have saved themselves a lot of trouble by focusing solely on the Netherlands. Because, interesting though ancient Egyptian culture is, everyone knows that if you want mysterious, prehistoric monuments you need to be in the province of Drenthe. There, more than fifty dolmens have survived, impressive memorials in stacked natural stone, some over twenty thousand kilograms in weight. Earthenware pots were among the things found in the tombs beneath the monuments, and these gave the builders the posthumous name of Funnelbeaker people. The dolmens are hundreds of years older than the pyramids at Giza.

And speaking of pyramids: the Netherlands has one of its own. It's built of sand and grass sods, it's true, but it is a real, twenty-metre-high pyramid. It is near the village of Austerlitz in the province of Utrecht and was built in 1804 on the initiative of the French commander of a Dutch-French army. The man intended to honour his leader, the infamous Napoleon B.

Like the pyramids of Egypt and America, this one is a source of inspiration for fans of grand symbolic vistas, also known as 'pyramidiots'. The pyramid was apparently in the exact centre of the country and specifically sited in relation to the Temple Mount in Jerusalem. It's interesting food for thought on your climb to the top, as in contrast to the pyramids of Giza you can get to the summit without being bothered.

Alright, the Netherlands might lack a Great Wall of China or a similar construction to keep the barbarian hordes at bay. It does, however, possess the most impressive dikes and dams in the world – it's just the same. And in comparison with the mystical ruined cities of Petra in Jordan and Machu Picchu in Peru, both of which are on the new worldwide list, there is a whole series of mysterious submerged villages, the most famous of which is the Drowned Land of Saeftinghe in Zeeland. Next, the famous statue of Christ in Rio de Janeiro: this has its counterpart in the statues of Hans Brinker, saviour *par excellence* of truly mythical proportions. Finally, the extraordinarily beautiful Taj Mahal in India and Roman Colosseum can be placed beside a no less impressive building: the former city hall of Amsterdam which was referred to as 'the eighth wonder of the world' back in the seventeenth century. Add to these the six Dutch contributions to the UNESCO World Heritage List, and there is really no reason why the whole of the Netherlands shouldn't be put on the list.

What else is there, you ask? You name it, it's here. You'd like to see an amusing leaning tower like the one in Pisa? The rugged Oldenhove in Leeuwarden is a good two metres out of plumb. Do you crave an impressive cathedral like that of Milan? The Dom Tower in Utrecht is hard to overlook at 112 metres. A Dutch 'city of lights', perhaps? How about Eindhoven, the birthplace of

Philips? A place divided in two, like Berlin once was and Nicosia still is? The old smugglers' village of Baarle is a real jigsaw puzzle of Dutch and Belgian enclaves. Do you want genuine mountains? The highest at Vaals pierces the clouds at 322 metres, and just like the similarly lofty Mount Everest, it is the point at which three countries meet. The big advantage of the Vaalserberg is of course that you can reach the peak in a couple of hours, and there is only a slight risk of altitude sickness, frozen body parts and an uncomfortable encounter with the Abominable Snowman.

All in all, the Netherlands is bursting with things to see. Tellingly, most Dutch people are at best halfway through discovering their country. It's a consoling thought, however, that if you get a move on you can see it all in about six months.

Where do we start? In Amsterdam, of course. There's a risk that you might end up staying for six months and missing the rest. You see, despite its small size (less than 750,000 inhabitants) Amsterdam is a major cosmopolitan city and is brimming with attractions. Sights of world renown includes the Rijksmuseum, with its unique collection of Golden Age paintings; the Rembrandt House Museum, where the master of painting lived and worked for almost twenty years; the Van Gogh Museum, with a stunning collection of works by Vincent and his illustrious contemporaries; and the Anne Frank House, the hiding place of the Jewish girl killed by the Nazis during the Second World War, along with ninety per cent of the Jewish community of Amsterdam. After the occupation, her diary was published as *The Diary of a Young Girl* and translated into more than sixty languages.

But Amsterdam is so much more than a sum total of sights to see. The city's attraction can be found particularly in the unique atmosphere you breathe as you wander along the canals and through the narrow streets of the historical city centre, with countless hidden monuments, a variety of cafés, restaurants and shops, and a population drawn from all corners of the globe – in 2007, 177 different nationalities lived in Amsterdam, more than in any other city in the world. Above all, it has an atmosphere of freedom, equality and tolerance, of civil liberalism, that in all its naturalness gives the city its exceptional character.

Blessed is the visitor with some power of imagination. He stands face to face with the Golden Age, the period in which the first signs of this mentality attached themselves to every new paving stone and bridge railing in the rapidly-growing trade metropolis. At the end of the sixteenth century, Amsterdam outshone the other powerful cities in the Low Countries and became the dynamo of the brand-new Republic of the Seven United Netherlands.

The wealth of Amsterdam came from trading with southern Europe, the Baltic region and Asia. The Asiatic trade in particular fires the imagination. It was the domain of the illustrious Dutch East India Company (VOC) established in 1602 – the first multinational and the first stock-exchange-listed company in the world. It set up hundreds of trading posts and forts on the Asiatic coasts. The trade in spices such as cloves, nutmeg and mace from the East Indies – present-day Indonesia – in particular earned a fortune.

In 1621, the VOC gained a sister who also made a significant contribution to Amsterdam's coffers: the Dutch West India Company (WIC). This enterprise set up trading posts along the entire west coast of Africa, the east coasts of North and South America and a number of Caribbean islands. The WIC gained notoriety for its part in the slave trade, but it was also involved in founding Amsterdam's namesake in the New World: New Amsterdam, capital of the colony of New Netherland, situated on the island of Manahatta (Manhattan). The island was bought in 1625 from the local Indians for a mound of trinkets – clothes, weapons and a cooking pot – to the value of sixty Dutch guilders. Forty years on from its founding, New Amsterdam was taken by the British. The Dutch won it back, but ultimately relinquished the city in exchange for Surinam. Even under the name of New York the city didn't fare too badly in the years to come.

All around the world, Dutch place and street names, forts and other remnants are testimony to these overseas adventures, which eventualy left the Netherlands with three colonies: the Dutch East Indies (now Indonesia), Surinam and the Netherlands Antilles. The first two became independent in the course of the twentieth century while the Antilles are still part of the Kingdom.

With Amsterdam as its nerve centre, the Dutch republic was the undisputed political, economic and cultural centre of the world between roughly 1600 and 1670. Modern capitalism first developed in this small, peculiar trading nation without a sovereign. The Bank of Amsterdam founded in 1609 became the most important financial institution in Europe. Innovations followed in quick succession in other sectors, too. Shipbuilding, cartography, the sciences and the arts saw unprecedented growth. Under the influence of these turbulent developments Amsterdam grew, literally, out of joint. The port was evocatively described as a 'forest of masts'. Between 1580 and 1675 the population grew from approximately 30,000 to over 200,000.

In order to deal with the growth, the city was considerably enlarged, including the famous belt of canals comprising the Herengracht, Keizersgracht and Prinsengracht. This is where wealthy, influential merchants built their stately canalside homes and warehouses which still define the look of the city centre today.

Amsterdam definitively became the 'Venice of the North', or as one foreign visitor expressed it, a 'water labyrinth'. The canals, by the way, were not only a blessing: an eighteenth-century visitor noted 'Amsterdam is a beautiful girl, but her breath stinks.'

As the jewel in the crown, the administrators of the city had the 'eighth wonder of the world' built: the largest city hall in Europe, a real temple of government to symbolise the power and wealth of Amsterdam. It was erected on the spot where, in the thirteenth century, the dam was built that gave Amsterdam its name. The grand building – now the Royal Palace – was a city hall, a court, a bank and a meeting place for citizens all in one. Many visitors are surprised at its drab, austere exterior. Why doesn't this wonder of the world have an imposing entrance, but seven small entrance gates? The builders wanted to emphasise that the city hall was of and for the people – it literally had to be a low-threshold building. The seven portals are a reference to that number of provinces which comprised the Republic. The typical Dutch ideal of equality was there early on.

However, the contrast with the interior is huge. The overwhelming decor of the *Burgerzaal* (reception room) poses Amsterdam as the centre of the world. Like other elements of the classicist building, the hall is based on the architecture of ancient Rome. It's impossible to misread its message: like Rome in its day, Amsterdam in the seventeenth century was the most powerful city in the world.

This power is still plainly visible in the city. The historical city centre is the largest of its kind in Europe. With nine thousand monuments, the biggest system of canals in the world and more bridges than any other city in Europe, Amsterdam is a real open air museum. A museum with an unmistakeable informal atmosphere that is all its own. Although some would sooner call it indifference, looking at the hundreds of nonchalantly moored houseboats on the canals and the thousands of even-more-sloppily-parked bicycles on the bridges. An atmosphere of freedom and tolerance which also guides many to one of the numerous coffeeshops or the Hash, Marihuana & Hemp Museum – the best place to learn more about the famous home-grown cannabis. Or, the popular Sex Museum and the notorious Red Light District with the unusual name of *De Wallen* (The Walls), which harks back to the city ramparts which were here during the fourteenth century.

And what about trading? The port of Amsterdam was overtaken long ago by that of Rotterdam, but is still the fourth largest in Europe. Of equal importance is Schiphol Airport just outside the city, one of the two exceptionally muscular showpieces of Dutch commerce. This ultra-modern 'mainport' is the fourth largest in Europe and is the home base of the Royal Dutch Airlines (KLM), the oldest airline still in operation in the world. The company merged with Air France in 2004. This move gave rise to fears that the company, which although it may not bear a cow on its tailfin was still seen as typically Dutch, would lose its identity. This worry was unfounded: the appearance of KLM planes is still as blue as the Dutch waters.

If Amsterdam has given you a taste for historical urban beauty, you'll be entertained for months. In the *Randstad* alone, the highly-urbanised region stretching southwards from Amsterdam, such medium-sized towns as Haarlem, Leiden, Delft, Gouda and Dordrecht are worth seeing. The other three large cities are also in this metropolitan area with its rural 'Green Heart': the attractive Utrecht, the dignified administrative centre of The Hague, and ambitious Rotterdam. Each of these is rooted deep in the past, though little can be seen of this in Rotterdam. The city, the second largest in the Netherlands (almost 600,000 inhabitants), was largely devastated by German bombing during the Second World War.

This dire fate defined the future of Rotterdam. With incredible perseverance, the post-war inhabitants made a virtue of necessity, in accordance with *'Geen woorden, maar daden'* ('No words but deeds'), the club anthem of the renowned Rotterdam football club, Feyenoord, traditional rival of Amsterdam Ajax. The city rose like a phoenix from the ashes but the renewal bug never left the people of Rotterdam. It became a field for architectural experiments which came much later in other parts of the Netherlands. It gave Rotterdam the reputation of the most modern and dynamic city in the country, an image that is best expressed by a classic joke: ask a Rotterdam local what the building across the street is, and he answers, 'No idea, it wasn't there yesterday.'

The many unusual and, by Dutch standards, towering buildings are the reason why the city has been dubbed 'Manhattan on the Maas' by the Dutch. Internationally, too, Rotterdam regularly attracts attention with daring architectural jewels such as the elegant Erasmus Bridge, named after the fifteenth-century humanist, a beloved 'son of the city'.

Equally beloved are the old architectural showpieces which survived the bombardments, such as the intimate wharfs of Delfshaven, which will forever be associated with the Pilgrim Fathers. At the beginning of the seventeenth century these strict English Protestants sought refuge in the Dutch Republic but decided in 1620 to create their own paradise in North America. The group sailed from Delfshaven to Plymouth in England, from where they and a number of kindred souls set a course for the promised land.

Their example was followed by many over the centuries, albeit that many later emigrants were driven not by religious but economic motives. The handsome Hotel New York is a tangible reminder of this, situated in the former headquarters of the renowned Holland-America Line. After the Second World War, hundreds of thousands of Dutch people sailed towards a new future with this company. In 1952 alone seventy-six thousand Dutch people left their homeland.

Nowadays, the number of passengers in the famous port of Rotterdam is far surpassed by the stacks of containers and goods which are stored and shipped there. Mainport Rotterdam is, after Shanghai and Singapore, the third largest port in the world, and like Schiphol it is a showpiece of the Dutch economy. The harbour stretches out forty kilometres from the centre of the city into the North Sea. If it's up to the port barons, future expansion awaits there in the form of another large, man-made peninsula.

The development plan for the harbour has been squabbled over for years. No Dutch person is averse to prosperity, but in a country where space is one of the most precious commodities, mega-projects are by definition subjected to sharp scrutiny. Won't this harm the countryside? What about pollution? Whether you are talking about the Port of Rotterdam, Schiphol Airport, the establishment of gigantic wind farms or a new national airport on islands in the North Sea – the commonsensical minds become overheated at the sight of the initial sketches. Economic necessity versus habitability: it's an old Dutch dilemma.

And the result is often just as Dutch. Once all interested parties have crossed swords in endless procedures and have fought out their conflicts at the highest level, the project is realised in modified form. The compromise generally involves all manner of environmental guarantees which will provide further fuel for conflict at a later stage, as they are not always honoured. Widespread indignation is the result, and amid much wringing of hands politicians eventually set up an enquiry into how this could have happened, although the answer is rarely satisfactory – the Dutch are not the best at recognising their own blunders.

This concern for the environment and the countryside is understandable given the rapid increase in the population over the last century – from five million inhabitants in 1900, to ten million by 1950, to the present-day 16.4 million. In particular, those living in villages in the west have in recent decades been shocked to see whole neighbourhoods of apartment blocks suddenly appear on the horizon. However, if you take the trouble to follow in the footsteps of the enthusiastic tourists of bygone centuries, you'll notice that there are still interesting and picturesque villages to be found, even in the west.

Many early tourists saw even then that a brief jaunt to the famous Dutch towns was not sufficient to get to know the country. In the countryside they claimed they had found the 'real Holland', where the noble savage still lived according to his authentic traditions and where the skyline was not besmirched with rows of windmills and other modern nonsense. They were in their element in such villages as Volendam and Broek in Waterland, with their smart timber houses which reminded them of big dolls' houses. An international artists' colony developed in the isolated fishing village of Volendam in the late nineteenth century. Painters and photographers swarmed around the startled fishermen in their peculiar costumes, which they gaily immortalised in romantic depictions. A sign was hung on the front of the only hotel in the village bearing the legend 'Welcome, artists'.

But time did not stand still even in Volendam. Younger villagers started to wear modern clothing and the artists complained that the people of Volendam started to live up to their clichéd image. The hotelier offered them consolation by setting up a room as an old-fashioned Volendam sitting-room. This kept the artists busy for a while with models dressed up as authentic villagers.

These days, Volendam is known largely as the cradle of technically skilful football players, and singers with their own style and sound – the famous 'eel sound' even has its own museum: the Palingsound Museum. Along with nearby coastal spots like Marken and Edam, renowned for its cheese, Volendam is a permanent stop on the beaten path of coach tourism. Villagers in traditional costume are few and far between these days, but a solution to this has been found: the tourists are stuffed into fisherman outfits and the natives take the pictures.

The apprehension surrounding major economic projects is fuelled less by the fear that typical village culture will disappear completely, than by the threat they pose to the Dutch landscape. Foreigners are surprised by this anxiety. Viewed from the air, isn't the Netherlands surely a patchwork quilt of green, neatly-parcelled polders? Would it really be such a disaster were a parcel to be lost here and there?

The reality is a little more complicated. The Netherlands may be known for being one big pasture, but in fact the landscape is uncommonly varied. The hilly landscape of Limburg, the heaths of Drenthe, the Frisian lakes, the unique Frisian Islands, the ancient polders of the Green Heart, and a range of unusual agricultural landscapes demonstrate a surprising versatility. All of these landscapes have one thing in common: almost without exception, they are the product of human intervention. Just about the only untamed scenery is to be found here and there along the coast. This doesn't preclude the Dutch from generously referring to all the landscapes outside the cities as 'countryside', and being keen to protect them.

And, happily, there is plenty of that going on. The Netherlands has twenty national parks with unusual flora and fauna, some of which are extremely rare even by international standards. In addition, private organisations manage hundreds of nature reserves while the government has designated twenty large areas as 'national landscapes'. The intention is to connect these regions by buying up tracts of agricultural land between them and converting them into 'rugged countryside' through major human intervention. Since the Dutchman was first faced with the challenge of protecting his habitat and making it habitable, the idea that he can 'mend' the whole of society and even nature has never left him. For some years the Netherlands has had its own Environmental Assessment Agency to keep the countryside on the right track.

Beyond the national landscapes, the Dutch have also created 'new countryside' – popularly termed 'bulldozer countryside' – in many places, sometimes with species of plant and animal that had vanished from the Netherlands. As a result, European bison now roam the Kennemerduinen and families of beavers imported from Central Europe gnaw their way through the Millingerwaard.

In many of these 'returned-to-nature' areas, maintenance is left to animals put there specifically for the purpose. Go to just about any nature reserve and you will meet a couple of wild Scottish Highland cattle passing their days as unpaid gardeners. Polish konik horses and Scottish Galloway cattle have also been

integrated fully into the Dutch countryside. Tourists are sometimes scared silly by such wild apparitions. But an answer to this
has also been found. Information meetings are sometimes given
to familiarise holidaymakers with the instruction manuals for
these animals, so that they can enjoy their journey of discovery
through the Dutch wilderness without concern.

No self-respecting tourist can leave the Netherlands without
finding out about the ancient struggle against water, and of course
the water itself. With regard to the former, the mighty Delta works
are the place to be. A trip across the islands of Zeeland and Zuid-
Holland will provide a decent impression of the immense project,
but if you want to find out the details you need to visit the former
artificial island of Neeltje Jans – part of the massive storm flood
barrier on the Oosterschelde in the province of Zeeland. This is
the location of the Deltapark, a theme park with exhibitions on
the Delta works and the historical war on water, and a number of
attractions for water rats and landlubbers alike.

Crossing one of the large rivers by ferry is an excellent way to
get to know the impressive river landscape, immortalised by Hendrik Marsman in his poem *Herinnering aan Holland (Memories of
Holland)*, which starts with the famous line: 'Thinking about Holland, I see broad rivers moving slowly through endless lowlands.'
Of course, this wonderful world of water also offers many other
opportunities to become acquainted with the stuff: try a boat trip
on the IJsselmeer or one of the countless other lakes, hire a sail-
ing or rowing boat on one of the many ponds or get aboard a trip
round the harbours of Rotterdam or Amsterdam.

Sportier holidaymakers can have a go at mudflat-walking;
unusual walks across boggy areas of the flats under the supervision of a guide. An outing like this is worth combining with a

visit to one of the Frisian Islands. Don't pay any attention to the weather charts in the media, which often dump a rain cloud over Texel due to a shortage of space, even when the island is basking in the sun's rays. The island's authorities have protested strongly against this shady practice.

Finally, if you wish to wage your own war on water, in keeping with Dutch tradition, grab a bucket and spade and head for the beach. Ignore the fellow tourists who seem to want to dig holes – that's not how you build a dike. Should you require reinforcements, there are always children around who will be happy to explain how to build an impregnable sandcastle.

GETTiNG
6THeRE
IS hALF THe FUN

But how do I get to the middle of nowhere?

Foreign visitors arriving at Schiphol after a tiring flight don't generally feel like tackling public transport straight away: they get a taxi to their destination. First find a hotel and a Heineken, you hear them think, then we'll see. Sometimes, foreigners are just like the Dutch.

The taxi ride is not always the pleasant introduction to the Netherlands they may have hoped for. In fact, tourists complain about Dutch taxis in all kinds of ways. You regularly hear of the smartly-dressed cabbies being less than courteous, bordering on rude. If you're unlucky, you might even find yourself involved in a blinding row between an unlicensed taxi driver and an official taxi driver at Schiphol. And, as if the fares weren't high enough, some drivers maintain a highly creative pricing policy. Drivers who manage to pass off the selected frequency on the car radio as the fare surely deserve a mention in the *Guinness Book of World Records*. But you can't blame their customers for objecting.

Such practices are hardly unique, as anyone who has ever used a taxi at an airport or in a large city anywhere else in the world knows. But in a country that is already roughly halfway up the ladder of civilisation, you'd expect different. Luckily, there are plenty of decent alternatives in Dutch towns. In some, you can even travel by rickshaw or *tuk-tuk*. Otherwise, you can just use the bus, tram or underground. You can even buy a card that allows access to all these modes of transport. Nothing could be more convenient or modern, you might say.

'You need a stripping card,' I once heard a helpful Amsterdam native say to a smartly-dressed Japanese family, who looked as lost at a tram stop as castaways on a desert island. From the ensuing unintelligible conversation it appeared that the essence of the message had not got across quite right. The Japanese disappeared into a taxi, still unaware of the convenience of the *nationale strippenkaart* available everywhere.

If even the local transport is so pitfall-prone, they must have asked themselves later in desperation, how on earth are we going to get to the bulb fields tomorrow? How do we avoid being dumped unceremoniously in Sexbierum? Judging by the name, it sounds like a place where you're likely to end up in a maelstrom of wickedness even without a 'stripping card'.

If you want to spare yourself such worries, you'll have to hire a car. There's something to be said for this for other reasons too: compared to taxi fares, the cost is surmountable and the intricate Dutch road network is much better and safer than some self-appointed experts attest. Moreover, it's the best way to be a Dutchman among the Dutch. Around three-quarters of all the mileage travelled in the Netherlands is done by car. Almost half of all Dutch people own such a vehicle. A Dutch adult without a car can expect to be regularly looked on with pity and the handful of Dutch people who do not hold driving licences are pointed at and mocked in the street.

The result is as you'd expect: a significant proportion of the population is stuck in traffic queues every day, either resigned or smouldering with irritation. Statisticians claim that in 2006, the Dutch spent over forty-four million hours in traffic jams. To avoid the ever-growing processions on the roads, many Dutch people have no choice but to get out on the road before daylight.

For decades, experts have thought, brainstormed and convened with might and main to find a solution to the traffic problem. One drastic measure after another is kicked around but improvements seem a long way off. What is certain is that you won't get Dutch people out of their cars for love or money. Just as in other well-off countries, the car is more sacred than the dairy producer of the meadows, which is pretty popular itself in the Netherlands.

Of course, tourists are lucky enough to be able to avoid the morning and evening rush hours, although that is slowly becoming scant comfort: the likelihood of ending up in a different traffic jam grows by the day. Furthermore, in many towns there are parking problems which seem impossible to solve. In the big cities in particular, parking is a nerve-wracking and expensive activity.

What else can be said about the Dutch road and car culture? Quite a few Dutch people think the maximum speed of 120 kilometres per hour should be a lot higher. They reckon that this snail pace is ridiculous: even when you're not in a traffic jam you're barely moving forward. If you want to really put your ride through its paces, you have to cross the border. Germany isn't the most popular country with the Dutch, but at least you can put your foot down there. So tourists who like to drive fast know where they should spend their holiday savings.

All in all, driving in the Netherlands is not an unconfined joy. But then, drivers sigh, what's the alternative? Public transport? Don't make me laugh. It would take me even longer on that cattle transport. And I'd have to stand up, too.

Complaining about public transport is even more popular than complaining about traffic queues, but in comparison with most other countries the Netherlands has had an excellent public transport system for centuries. Around 1600, ships sailed over frozen lakes on runners at speeds that made passengers' hair stand on end. If the waterways were not frozen solid, the passenger would travel at a more moderate pace by track boat. Thanks to the widely-branching network of canals, the Netherlands in the seventeenth century had a transport system that was for its time astonishingly efficient and modern. However, during the nineteenth century the track boat had become the symbol of Dutch inertia and backwardness. It was time for a great leap forward, and that's what happened: in 1839 the first train puffed its way from Amsterdam to Haarlem, although it would take several more decades before the country had a truly modern rail network.

'Fast, safe and affordable' was, for a long time, the slogan used by the Nederlandse Spoorwegen railway (NS) to attract passengers.

After a number of train hijackings in the nineteen-seventies, not even the most fanatical train enthusiast dared utter the phrase. Even today, the NS still attracts the scorn of the population. The company has to suffer criticism by the truckload: the trains are too full, they regularly fail to run on time, and every five minutes there is a computer or overhead line malfunction causing a series of train breakdowns. The absurdity continues when the NS' excuses for winter delays involve leaves nonchalantly falling onto tracks or snowflakes which have the cheek to lodge themselves in points. It's easy to arrive at a creative interpretation of the initials 'NS': National Shame.

Is it really that bad? There's no doubt that some of the rolling stock is due for replacement, that waiting passengers are often left in the cold regarding delays, that there's a very good chance you won't find a seat during rush hour, and that there are not many who spend an hour standing up in a crammed carriage for fun, with anyone who does being either insane or up to no good.

Even so, with the train you can still go places. Not only is the rail network intricate, it is also very busy – the Netherlands, along with Japan and Switzerland, leads the world in this regard. Furthermore, 85 per cent of trains run on time, an achievement that is equalled in few other countries, and in general NS staff are helpful and polite: the inspectors still ask decorously for *plaatsbewijzen'* (proof of seating entitlement) rather than *kaartjes* (tickets).

Things can get difficult if you need to get to the proverbial middle of nowhere. It's a good idea to take a sandwich to eat on the way. On this type of route, not even the very respectable intercity bus transport offers any comfort. These days, lines to sparsely-populated and rarely-visited places are, in transport jargon, 'uneconomic'. The NS tries to soften the blow by making larger stations more like shopping and entertainment precincts at which, coincidentally, the odd train stops from time to time. Following on from the successful Airport City concept at Schiphol Airport, stations are to become 'gateways to the city'; fun places to be for even the most profoundly frustrated traveller.

All in all, public transport is not half as bad as many Dutch people would have you believe, and especially not in comparison with other countries. And there's another major difference with the rest of Europe: apart from a hardcore of car addicts, the Dutchman gets on his bike if at all possible. The Netherlands is the number one country for cycling: a land of intrepid pedallers. There are at least twenty million examples of this convenient mode of transport in circulation, and as such the Netherlands enjoys the highest bicycle density in the world by some distance. The close bond between the polder dweller and the bicycle is renowned the world over, and takes on all but mythical proportions, as demonstrated by the relief of a cycling Dutchman in a Hindu temple on the island of Bali, once part of the colonial island kingdom of the Dutch East Indies.

The matter of how the bicycle became a Dutch symbol of indomitability is one best left to ambitious scientists. What is certain is that the bicycle is not a Dutch invention, but a British or French one. But, while the enthusiasm for the two-wheeler never grew brighter than a pilot flame in those countries, the Netherlands' passion for cycling reached campfire levels. Indubitably, the flatness of the landscape played a part in this, but there are other regions which meet this criterion where locals would think you mad for suggesting a cycling trip. In the Netherlands, however, babies are put on three-wheelers before they can even talk: on your bike!

For foreigners who love 'going native', the iron horse is a gift from above. When you hire a bike you are already integrated, up to saddle height, before you mount. The rest does demand some concentration and practice. Cyclists wobbling through the traffic are immediately exposed as pseudo-Dutch.

Therefore, you should not immediately hire the trendiest bike but a simpler model without whistles and just the one bell. Such contraptions are known as *omafiets* (grandmother's bicycle), although bicycle manufacturers tend to wrap the elderly in cotton wool these days with electric motors and other trickery. The modern city bikes, all terrain bikes and other models with which manufacturers appeal to the fashion and identity-conscious cyclist are more attractive, but operating advanced gears in combination with manual brakes can be detrimental to more elementary skills such as keeping the handlebars straight. The *omafiets* has but one fancy gadget: the hub brake, unheard of in many countries.

Another aid on the cycle path to Dutchness is wearing a long, chunky chain with a sturdy padlock around the shoulders. It is a subtle code indicating that you are a seasoned cyclist.

In the larger towns in particular, the chain is an essential attribute. Away from the home, the Dutch chain their bikes to lampposts, trees, bus stops, fences and bridge railings. A million bikes are sold every year but 750,000 are stolen – thankfully rarely with the rider attached. In the course of his life, the average Dutchman will lose four bicycles in this way. The Netherlands can also boast the highest bike theft density in the world.

The majority of thieves by far belong to the guild of junkies, who view the theft of a couple of bikes as an effective means of buying drugs. These stolen bikes are sold at knock-down prices.

In order to check this miserable tradition, the government has recently set up a hotline for stolen bicycles. The idea is to reduce the number of thefts by a hundred thousand per year. To be honest, the junkies are not losing any sleep over it.

Apart from thieves and all forms of motorised traffic, there are a few other hazards which threaten the cyclist's welfare. Many cyclists only notice that the bicycle wheel fits perfectly into a tram rail when it is too late. Such experiences usually end up in Casualty. And there are also a few million cycling anarchists. The model type cycles without using hands and without lights at night, does not ring his bell when overtaking or indicate before turning into a side street, and slaloms through traffic as he pleases, carrying a heavy load all the while. Visitors are often astounded at what one can carry on a bike. For example, a couple of dogs tucked cosily into a handlebar basket, or a cluster of kids – on the crossbar, handlebar, back or arm, standing or sitting on the back or in a homemade trailer or pushcart. Long ago, the English writer Aldous Huxley described how 'the most daring masterpieces of the circus and variety theatre are part of everyday life in Amsterdam.'

Cyclists – and also pedestrians – who are not used to this silent mode of transport are regularly scared out of their skin. Happily, the Dutch are well used to foreigners who are not used to bikes. Cases have been known in which men have allowed themselves to be run into by shapely women on bicycles so that they can help them to their feet afterwards. It's a sure-fire winner, some claim, but there is the risk that the first woman you meet following a collision is the nurse lifting your plaster-encased leg in a pulley.

Once you're familiar with the basic principles of bike culture, you'll find that cycling is a relaxing activity and that not even the busy, complex city centres are really traffic jungles where the survival of the fittest reigns. With an abundance of traffic lights, signs, zebra crossings and speed bumps, the system aims, according to good Dutch practice, to allow all road users optimum protection and opportunities to express themselves without getting under the wheels of the rest of the traffic. The cyclist enjoys privileges in the form of his own traffic lights, cycle racks at stations and shopping malls, and best of all, his own nationwide road network in the form of twenty-thousand kilometres of cycle path.

Thanks to this network, the bicycle is not only an excellent means of getting to the middle of nowhere, but also of 'doing' the whole country. No problems with traffic jams, delays, rude taxi drivers or stripping cards. Furthermore, some of the cycle paths cross nature reserves which are not accessible to motorised traffic. There are few countries where the possibilities are so great for giving real meaning to the famous travellers' motto 'Getting there is half the fun'.

Throughout the land, cycle routes both long and short have been laid out through the most beautiful scenery, past the loveliest sights and around every theme imaginable. For example, anyone wishing to gain an impression of the centuries-long struggle against water can choose between coastal routes, routes around the IJsselmeer, through the 'new land' – the IJsselmeer polders – and along the border between the low and 'high' Netherlands. Any foreigner who completes such a route without suffering cramp or a tyre puncture surely deserves a mention in the *Guinness Book of World Records*.

The 7 ORANgE MACHINe

The undisputed number two

If there's one area in which the austere Dutch let themselves go, sometimes embarrassingly so, it's football. From time to time, the Netherlands makes a decent fist of it on the hallowed international turf and the millions of 'experts' are happy to explain why that is so, as dedicated apostles of the Dutch 'model'. Foreigners who have to deal with the Dutch should be particularly mindful of the fact that they will be initiated sooner or later into the obstinate views of the Dutch on the higher art of football: take heed, thy practitioners of park football, thy plodding ignoramuses, *this* is how the game should be played! Although the work of the world-famous Nederlands Dans Theater, Rembrandt's masterpieces and even the invention of the Daffodil with its 'smart gearstick' rarely, if ever, led to boisterous jingoism, it seems that such a thing as national passion really does exist when it comes to football.

This sentiment thrives partly because of the many commendations of foreign football experts and supporters. Even countries which passionately devote themselves to the immediate and permanent sinking of the Dutch abortion and cannabis boats, preferably with as many euthanasia doctors as possible on board, extol the virtues of Dutch football remarkably often. In fact, the Dutch national team enjoys unconditional admiration, or even a mild form of idolatry, everywhere football is viewed as the essence of human existence – that is, as everyone knows, every country in the world with the exception of Vatican City. The awe is such that the team is invariably reckoned as favourites at major tournaments, even if the players themselves haven't been able to hit a barn door for months.

In rural Mexico, a jolly, middle-aged Indian woman has no difficulty explaining why this is so. Indicating her rotund figure, she draws, in broken English, a comparison with the second national passion: *'Eet eez all about ze taste and beauty of ze game, you understand? Like food! The Holland team eez... hmm... how you say... plays tasteful and beautiful. Like a machine! La Naranja Mecánica!'*

La Naranja Mecánica – the Orange Machine. The expression trips off her tongue with a poetry that does justice to the playing style she describes: creative, dynamic, attacking football, garnished with technical feats. She'll miss a meal for it if she has to.

Alright, the machine stalls sometimes, perhaps more often than she will admit to, but the Dutch team at least tries to play neatly and attractively and entertain the crowd. And you can't say that about most other major football nations, which she goes on to sum up in a stream of heartfelt profanity punctuated with a few *carambas*. Who said the Indians were introverted?

The foundations of the boundless popularity of Dutch football were laid in the nineteen-seventies by Amsterdam's Ajax. Under the guidance of coach Rinus Michels, nicknamed 'the General', a strategic concept was developed within this legendary team which would become known as 'total football'. Its main characteristic was the dominant, attacking style, executed by at least three attackers who also defended and defenders who also attacked – a style of play that was every bit as frivolous and adventurous as the colour orange in which the national team plays.

The 'great Ajax' won three European Cups in a row and the Dutch team stole the show at the 1974 World Cup with the same concept, only to lose in the final needlessly to the host country and arch-rivals, Germany. The hangover was bad, but the Orange Machine had established its reputation. Four years later they lost another World Cup final, this time in and against Argentina. This defeat brought the national team the title of 'undisputed number two'. The hangover was only shaken off at the 1988 European Championships in Germany when 'Oranje' beat the home country first and then went on to win.

This title was celebrated not only as an ode to what was known in the Netherlands as the *Hollandse School* (Dutch School), but also as a 'second liberation day'. References to the Second World War could be seen earlier on in the tournament, such as banners bearing the legend 'Grandma, we've got your bike back'. This slogan, incomprehensible for foreigners, referred to the German occupation (1940-1945), when the invaders confiscated large numbers of bicycles. The relief in 1988 cleared the way for the normalisation of emotional relations with the Germans. To the first post-war generation in the Netherlands, these emotions were marked for a long time by the horrors of the occupation years. I can remember the indignant feelings which took over my youth team in the game against a German team during an international football tournament, which we won magnificently. Like a runaway orange steamroller we played the Germans *kaputt* and, as a bonus, we spat a hateful *'Noch ein Tor!'* in the faces of our dumbfounded German contemporaries every time a goal was scored. No wonder that the Germans never adopted the concept of total football.

Our neighbours to the east are not alone. Outside of the Netherlands, total football barely got a look in. The system with wing attackers, known as '4-3-3', is seen as attractive but risky, and the latter doesn't appeal much to anyone in football circles. In the moneyed world of football, the result is sacred and the emphasis is placed on a hermetically-sealed defence. Exceptions are rare, and are almost always the result of Dutch involvement. The Netherlands swims resolutely alone against the current.

The most prominent ambassador of the daring Dutch playing style is the most famous Dutchman in the world: Johan Cruijff. He is the steadfast guardian of the Hollandse School. During his playing career, Cruijff – it's no coincidence that his initials are JC – was the elegant inspiration and undisputed leader of the great Ajax and Dutch team, a role he next took on with fervour at Barcelona, where he was idolised as *El Salvador*, 'the Saviour'. The legendary 'Number 14' – a reference to the unusual shirt number that he started wearing in 1970 on his return to the pitch from long-term injury – was considered by many to be the greatest footballer of all time. His only rivals of note are the Brazilian Pelé, Argentina's Maradona and the German Beckenbauer. In Europe, he was voted footballer of the century.

Once his career as a player was over, Cruijff was a sensation as coach at Ajax and Barcelona. He moulded both clubs according to his attacking insights with great success. In Barcelona, he was celebrated as the restorer of Catalan self-awareness by breaking the hegemony of the hated arch-rival Real Madrid and helping the club achieve its first European Cup win. Today, he presides over a training institute where top sportspersons are prepped for management positions in the sports world, as well as the Johan Cruijff Foundation, a charitable institution which sets up sports and play projects for underprivileged children all over the world.

But above all else, as a newspaper columnist and match analyst on the national channel he is a tireless champion of 4-3-3. In his commentary he shows himself to be as much of a virtuoso as he had been with the ball at his feet: Cruijff turned out to be a reluctant linguistic innovator. His famous expression 'Every disadvantage has its advantage' is now a standard Dutch idiom. His 'Their defence was like a goat's cheese' slip of the tongue was priceless. Cruijff's trademark is his miraculous logic, which manifests itself in expressions such as 'Italians can't beat you, but you can lose to them', and 'Playing football is simple, but the hardest thing is to play simple football'. The standard addition of 'So that's logical' ought to dispel any doubt of the profound wisdom behind 'Cruijffisms'. They earned Cruijff a new nickname: the Oracle.

Cruijff's dogged missionary work has had unmistakeable results. In his own country, the principles of the Hollandse School are upheld by a large number of professional clubs. At Ajax, by far the most successful Dutch club, 4-3-3 is sacred. Woe betides the trainer who dares to announce new-fangled defensive tactics at the Amsterdam ArenA, the beautiful stadium which has earned the nickname of 'the sod hut' due to the pitiful condition of the playing surface. He definitely won't be able to show his face in the coffeeshop again.

Ajax players are brought up with the 'house style', as 4-3-3 is known in Amsterdam, at the famous youth training school which guarantees a continuous flow of talent, something that the Netherlands isn't short of anyway. The great tragedy, which also affects the other top clubs – PSV, Feyenoord and AZ – is that the most talented players are often snapped up at a young age by cash-rich soccer businesses in other European countries. The Netherlands has become used to the exodus of stars to Italy, Spain, England and Germany. The fact that the country's own top clubs are condemned, almost by definition, to a role as undisputed number two in the European arena is grudgingly accepted.

At present, Real Madrid, with four Dutch players in its ranks, is celebrated in Spain as the 'Orange Machine'. Other Southern European superpowers have also benefited from their Dutch colonies in the past: Barcelona, with Cruijff and Neeskens, later Koeman and even half of the Dutch national team; and AC Milan, with the *tulipani* – tulips – Van Basten, Gullit and Rijkaard. A remarkable number of these former migrant workers are now employed as trainers in foreign climes. Dutch trainers are in as much demand as the top players.

However, some individuals have also been able to make their mark on the playing styles of foreign teams. Dennis Bergkamp, who has since retired, was trained at Ajax and briefly wasted away at the defensive Internazionale, before being celebrated as a vital artist at Arsenal. Bergkamp was a typical product of the Hollandse School: elegant, artistic, focused and blessed with great insight. As a team-mate at Arsenal explained accurately: 'As the ball was coming to him, he had already scored the goal.' The modest attacker was known in England as 'the non-flying Dutchman' due to his fear of flying, though more commonly he was known as the 'Dutch Master'.

Even so, the player who has won the most prestigious prizes is not Cruijff, his disciples Van Basten and Bergkamp, or the stylish powerhouses Gullit and Rijkaard, but Clarence Seedorf. The midfielder has won the Champions' League four times with Ajax, Real Madrid and AC Milan, and no one Dutch player can hold a candle to that. The muscular Surinamese rough diamond debuted with Ajax at the age of sixteen and created history during a post-match television interview. The reporter asked whether he had seen Franz Beckenbauer, who had flown in specially, before the match. Yes, Seedorf confirmed with a chuckle, in the catacombs of the stadium before taking the field. It was quite an honour; Mr Beckenbauer is a living football legend after all, isn't he?

Then it happened.

'We nutmegged him,' said Seedorf, grinning from ear to ear.

'Nutmegged him?!' spluttered the journalist. You... Mr Beckenbauer... *Kaiser* Franz... you kicked the ball between his feet?!'

'Yes, he walked up towards us. Then we just nutmegged him.' Seedorf said it as if he had just let the dog out.

Clarence couldn't go wrong from then on. He had stolen my heart forever, even though he later became more difficult to love by turning the missing of penalties into a fine art. He made a habit of hoofing the ball with thunderous force into the furthest stand at crucial moments. He would often demand the ball in order to finish off the job – which does say something about his sense of responsibility – and it earned him the scorn of the Dutch public. This caused him to make a statement during his years of service at AC Milan which made everything alright again: 'It's time to stop all these questions about penalties. They never ask about it here in Italy, even though I always miss here, too.'

The negative comments regarding Seedorf are typical of the unusually critical attitude of Dutch football fans. They are passionate, but also spoilt and demanding, bordering on unreasonable. Unlike elsewhere in the world, good results are not enough: one is expected to play good football! The young national coach, Marco van Basten, must look back with nostalgia at his glory years in Italy, where he was revered as *San Marco* and was carried on the shoulders of his team-mates after a bloodless but welcome 0-0 score. Now he experiences first-hand how high the expectations of the Dutch are. He achieves good results and the Dutch team is, as usual, among the top sides in the FIFA world rankings, but the stars' performances are regularly below-par, and as a result Saint Marco is often subjected to criticism. He knows all too well what this can lead to. In 2004, his predecessor Dick Advocaat, the 'Little General', was hounded from the national football stage with his tail between his legs after a fatal substitution during the European Championships.

It is also typical that the Netherlands is one of the few countries in the world where the expression 'the Orange Machine' is rarely used. There is no need to emphasise that the team operates like a well-oiled attacking machine: that goes without saying to the millions of Oranje fans. Just imagine, being satisfied with anything less! That's not why we take to the streets on important match days, jumping around disguised as oranges!

For the Dutch, football is a rare national passion. In the run-up to the major tournaments in which the Dutch team takes part, an Oranje tsunami floods the country, colouring everything in its path without prejudice. Buildings, streets and squares are concealed behind streamers and banners, window displays scream at you from afar, festive football songs blare from the bars, shopkeepers cannot stock up on Oranje cake, Oranje pudding and Oranje sprinkles fast enough and manufacturers ride the tidal wave with a deluge of humorous headwear, slippers, flags, horns, stickers ('Collect them all!') and all manner of trinkets. The media is also swept up in orange fever. Outside of the special football supplements and the extra radio and television broadcasts, it seems the world has ground to a halt. Only a small minority of Dutch people bravely, but ultimately in vain, put up resistance. Shaking their heads they hide away in their homes. Some opt for voluntary exile abroad.

Regardless of the current condition of the Orange Machine, the same question is brought up by orange-tinted television presenters before every World Cup: will Holland become world champions this time? The crystal ball says no, but after thorough analysis of the individual class and potential wizardry of the top Dutch players, of sketchy historical parallels and of the state of decline in which rivals currently find themselves, the experts – and there are a few million of them in the Netherlands – arrive at the opposite conclusion.

Even so, the almost unavoidable elimination of Oranje does not usually lead to a national nervous breakdown or depression. As if by magic, sobriety returns to heads and streets. The orange decorations disappear like snow in summer, the exiles return to society and after the collective excitement the nation focuses again on the order of the day. 'That was all they could do, which is what I've been saying all along,' is the prevailing view.

That is, as long as Oranje remains loyal to the principles of the Hollandse School. As long as the team plays with daring, artistry and attack, the way football was meant to be. If it neglects its duty, the wrath of Oranje will descend on the heads of players, trainers, coaches, bigwigs and anyone else within a kilometre's range of the Dutch Football Association headquarters. Games in which the Orange Machine does not function as it should offer the unique opportunity to see the Dutch through open curtains, screaming at their television with fists clenched: 'Profiteers!' Not even a victory can mollify the indignity.

An attacking, tactically-aware game is the benchmark, not only for professionals but also amateurs. With more than a million players, amateur football is an inexhaustible reservoir of talent. The term 'amateur football' should generally be taken with a pinch of salt. It's a public secret that in the higher regions, sumptuous 'expenses' are paid which give many players reason to switch clubs.

The most successful amateur club is the illustrious IJsselmeervogels (IJsselmeer Birds) from the fishing village of Bunschoten-Spakenburg, playing in the amateur first division. It's a fascinating club, if only for its wonderful name. In your imagination you can see the contemplative founder standing on a dike in a crashing storm, wet hair plastered to his face, when suddenly, in its silvery-white splendour, a large bird blows past. Eureka! The truth is less poetic: the club was formed by a merger of two older clubs, IJsselmeer and Strandvogels (Beach Birds). How come so many Dutch clubs have adopted the names of birds, real or imagined? Zeevogels (Sea Birds), Rijnvogels (Rhine Birds), Zuidvogels (South Birds), Watervogels (Water Birds), Zwaluwen Vooruit (Swallows Ahead) – this is another inexhaustible reservoir. The most powerful name is, without a doubt, Stormvogels (Fulmars). A name like a Dutch dike. Before the opponent takes the field, he knows: we're onto a hiding here. It's a different matter when you play against the Zangvogels (Songbirds) or the Dodos.

One way or another, you get the idea that IJsselmeervogels is one big family. Since time immemorial, a large proportion of the players have borne the name of De Graaf. During the week, the De Graafs travel around the Dutch markets with their fish and bread stalls, while on Saturdays the first team step onto the battlefield as one family.

The most famous scion of the De Graaf dynasty was Jaan. He made it as far as the premier division and gained cult status by never playing on a Sunday. The Presbyterian Bunschoten-Spakenburg is the jewel in the crown of the Dutch Bible Belt and the Sabbath is holy. This is why IJsselmeervogels play in the Saturday league. Even so, several professional clubs courted the favour of Jaan 'never on a Sunday' de Graaf. They usually played on Sundays, but also often on Saturdays and on those occasions Jaan would tear across the turf like a young lion.

IJsselmeervogels' great rival is the neighbouring club Spakenburg, which was previously named Stormvogels and Windvogels; yet more birds. The two clubs are adjacent to each other and there is no doubt that there are family connections which link them, but on the field they are anything but intimate. When the 'Blues' (Spakenburg) play the 'Reds' (IJsselmeervogels), blood is spilt all over the pitch. The day after the derby, the survivors sit brotherly next to each other in church.

The obvious question is whether there is such a thing as a Hollandse School in other sports? There certainly is. There are even sports which were invented in the Netherlands and are played so little in foreign countries that world titles are bestowed on the polder time and time again as a matter of course.

The best example is the noble korfball, a sport somewhat similar to basketball, which was dominated by the Netherlands from the very start. Korfball was introduced in 1902 by an Amsterdam teacher and is known in forty countries. However, in most of these the sport has never got past the embryonic stage. The Dutch korfballers only true rivals are their Belgian neighbours.

In spite of these successes, the sport suffers in its land of birth with limited interest and a stubborn image of frumpiness. This is undeserved, as not only is korfball fast and dynamic, it is also a sport in which men and women play together in the same team. It is the most emancipated sport in the world, and in that sense, a typical Dutch invention.

This is in stark contrast with ice skating, the only sport which remotely approaches football in popularity. At the first sign of frost, the Dutch head *en masse* for the skate sharpeners and flood entire fields, so that aficionados can get on the ice as quickly as possible. Once the country is fully in winter's grasp they swarm in their millions over canals, ponds and lakes. Races and tours are organised throughout the land. The impressive distances covered hark back to the time when skating was more of a necessity than a hobby. When the waterways froze over, skating was often the fastest and most practical means of getting from A to B.

The narrow blades were also successfully deployed by the Dutch during times of need. During the sixteenth-century Revolt against the Spanish, the defenders of the besieged city of Haarlem surprised their enemy by attacking on 'a board fitted with blades in order to stay on the ice without slipping and thus being able to walk and fight'. On hearing this alarming report from the battlefield, the Spaniards hastily ordered seven thousand pairs of skates, but when the soldiers found themselves requiring medical assistance as a result, the consignment was quickly dumped into a hole in the ice.

In competitive skating, it also seems that the Netherlands is not so much a country as a genuine skating nation. After the Dutch came back from a couple of defeats by Americans and a dastardly Italian who had craftily swiped a number of medals in recent competitions, a newspaper printed, in capitals: 'Skating nation the Netherlands restores order on ice rink'. It could not be any clearer.

Competitive skating has been dominated by the Dutch for years. Men in particular return to the proud fatherland from European and international championships with medals of honour. When the championships take place in the covered national temple of skating, Thialf in Heerenveen, the heroes are accompanied by a merry crowd clothed in comical orange costumes and a carnival band. You would be forgiven for forgetting that skating is an extremely serious and professional business, in which Dutch inventors lead the way in the development of new tricks which can shave precious hundredths of seconds from skaters' times.

The pinnacle of skating culture is the renowned yet notorious *Elfstedentocht*. This two-hundred-kilometre-long war of attrition through eleven Frisian towns is, due to its heroism, tragedy and the level of national excitement, an event that has no equal – a true popular festival. The skaters are driven on by oompa bands and hundreds of thousands of supporters from all corners of the land, swathed in orange and the blue and white of Friesland. If you attend an Elfstedentocht you can tackle the next ten years, so goes the conventional wisdom.

You'll need to, as well, as since the inception of this 'tour of tours' no more than fifteen have taken place, the last one in 1997. Pessimists predict that the tour is now a thing of the past. Creeping climate change means that the Netherlands is getting warmer, and in the long term it may even be reincarnated as a sun-kissed tourist destination. However, skating fans are keeping the faith. If Cruijff and his ilk can take on global football norms with their Hollandse School, beating climate change should be a cinch.

fAIRLy SToLEN

Traditional Dutch symbols

Ask a foreigner for his or her impression of the Netherlands and he or she will often bring up an impressive range of characteristics: the battle against the diabolical water, with the accompanying dikes and polders; the liberal drugs policy and other expressions of freedom and tolerance; the Golden Age painters who posthumously fill galleries; the tulips growing up to the sky; the sturdy but idyllic windmills; the cows which supply the country with its famous dairy products, and perhaps, even the essential Delft Blue souvenirs. The list of defining characteristics is a lengthy one, and this surfeit is a special characteristic in itself – especially for such a small country as the Netherlands. It's no wonder it's so low-lying, you might say.

Of course, the modern visitor is aware that not every Dutch person grows flower bulbs, drags a few sandbags up to the dike now and then, and sits down in the evening as high as a kite to decorate a Delft Blue ashtray with a brush made from cow's hair. However, what is less well known is that many of the afore-mentioned traditional Dutch symbols have as little to do with the Netherlands as a polar bear does with the Sahara. They fell into the laps of the Dutch years ago – as the Dutch would say, they were fairly stolen – and then became deeply embedded into polder culture. During this process they acquired their classical Dutch images and became world-renowned as such.

Take, for example, the clog, the ancient symbol of Dutch so-briety, determination, and also inventiveness; there can surely be no doubt that the wooden shoe was a godsend for the occupants of the boggy polders at the time. But is it a Dutch invention? No. As far as we know, the French can claim this honour, as the clog marched northwards from southern France up the Atlantic coast. The oldest Dutch clog dates back to the thirteenth century and was found in a dam that was built on the River Rotte around that time. The city of Rotterdam developed around this dam and the antique clog can be admired in that city's historical museum.

Once in Dutch hands – or more accurately, on Dutch feet – the French invention underwent a spectacular development. With the exception of the higher classes, the inhabitants of the Low Countries stepped wholesale into the modern footwear, which was filled up with straw during the winter as it still is today in the countryside. The materials required – willow and poplar wood – were in abundance and many of the wearers made their own clogs. Farmers would build up stocks during the quiet winter months, and some of these would also be sold.

However, manufacturing clogs was also a speciality, a craft that reached full stature in what is now the Netherlands. In the towns and cities during the fifteenth century, clogmakers organised themselves into guilds and, over time, regional variations appeared on the market. One could derive where each one had been made, or even its manufacturer, from looking at the shape, the use of colour or the motifs used to decorate it. Furthermore, in addition to the standard clog, wooden shoes were made for special occasions and activities: Sunday clogs for wearing to church, bridal clogs with woodcarvings, peat-cutters' clogs, ice clogs with spikes underneath, skating clogs, football clogs and even smugglers' clogs, which left prints which did not show the direction in which the wearer had gone but indicated the opposite direction.

Even in the era of modern communications, some foreigners think that nearly all Dutch people clatter around in wooden shoes, much as many westerners cherish the notion that all inhabitants of the interior of New Guinea wear penis gourds. It may be a surprise to learn that most Dutch people would be unable to set foot in them without breaking at least one leg. Farmers, gardeners and market traders in particular swear by the clog, for obvious reasons. It is also an essential item for folklore groups, especially if clog dancing is on the agenda.

Despite the great reduction in demand, clog production is flourishing like never before. A million are sold every year. After all, no self-respecting tourist wants to go home without a pair, whether they be a couple of mini-clogs on a keyring or a pair of warm slippers in the shape of clogs. As a dyed-in-the-wool trader, the Dutchman lovingly takes advantage of this. For example, he might replace the traditional decoration with modern folklore, such as a cannabis leaf, a hash-smoking farm girl, or – again, fairly stolen – the Nike logo. A handful of clog-making craftsmen benefit from tourism too, by giving demonstrations, with modest museums and of course an assortment of traditional Dutch footwear in all shapes and sizes.

The triumphal procession of the clog through the Low Countries can be compared to the development of another, apparently equally Dutch icon: the windmill. The general idea that windmills sprung forth from polder soil is, however, founded on quicksand. The mill probably originates from Iran, or travelled north via Spain from the Middle East or North Africa. Another disappointment is that there are countries with considerably more windmills than the Netherlands. That the Dutch, of all people, should have ended up as born millers in the collective consciousness is because they were able to exploit the possibilities of the machine introduced in the thirteenth century better than anyone else. Whereas the early windmills were used to grind corn, as were the watermills which had already long been in use, they quickly acquired many more uses and took on a main role in the development of the country as we now know it.

From the early fifteenth century onwards, the mill was deployed in the Mother of all Battles: the Dutch population's battle against water. With the help of the windmill, they were able to turn vast bodies of water into polders, and keep them drained as well. This was a decisive step in the development of the landscape as it is now. A step that could only be taken thanks to the inventiveness of the windmill builders and hydraulic engineers who designed the first 'polder mills' and went on to perfect the machinery in every way possible.

From the end of the sixteenth century, the windmills were also used for industrial purposes. In 1596, the first timber sawmill was erected in the Zaan district. The inventor presented his prototype in Amsterdam but was met with protest from the hand-sawers' guild, which saw its livelihood under threat. There were no such obstacles on the Zaan. The sawmill provided the impulse for fast and varied industrial development which turned the region into the first industrial zone in the world. The Zaan mills mixed paint, ground marble, beat hemp, pressed oil, pounded tobacco and milled pepper, lead, food and luxury goods such as cocoa, mustard and grain. By the mid-seventeenth century the district had six hundred mills, and a century later a thousand.

The Zaan district was particularly noted as a shipbuilding centre. Its shipyards were world-famous. In 1697 the Russian Tsar, Peter the Great, stayed undercover in Zaandam during his first trip to Western Europe in order to pick up some tips. The inquisitive Tsar, who had a special interest in this modern Holland and spoke reasonable Dutch, stayed in a simple timber house that is now a tourist attraction. The brand-new Russian capital he founded in 1703, Saint Petersburg, had strong Dutch influences: these included a system of canals and even a flourishing Dutch community, in which merchants from the small town of Vriezenveen held prominent positions. Shipyards were established in the centre on a site that was soon surrounded by canals, and from that moment on was also used as a timber store for the construction of the Russian fleet. The island is still called New Holland.

The Zaan development did not go unnoticed in the rest of the province of Holland. Industrial mills were quickly built in other cities. These were enormous monsters which towered high above all other buildings in order to catch enough wind. The prosperous Dutch Republic literally survived on wind in the seventeenth century. While its merchants sailed the world's seas plying their trade, polders were drained and all sorts of industry were kept running in the fatherland thanks to the windmill.

On the threshold of the steam age, the Netherlands had eleven thousand windmills. There are a thousand or so of these left, along with over a hundred watermills. A small number of them are in continuous operation. The oldest examples are two tower mills in Zevenaar and Zeddam, dating from the first half of the fifteenth century. The highest antique mill (at over forty-four metres, a world record) is called De Noord and can be found in Schiedam, where another four such giants are located within the city limits.

However, as a tourist attraction, these impressive works are no match for the eighteenth-century mill complex at Kinderdijk. Each year, millions of tourists gape at the nineteen polder mills connected in series, which until 1950 helped keep the impoldered Alblasserwaard dry. They are still in almost authentic condition.

Equally popular is the collection of industrial mills at Zaanse Schans in Zaandam. Most of the seven mills and the accompanying traditional craft businesses from the seventeenth and eighteenth century originally come from other parts of the Zaan district. They were rebuilt at Zaanse Schans. The Dutch do not mind shifting their heritage around in order to preserve it. Mills are still moved around from time to time. Almost all these colossal machines are now registered as monuments, although the existence of many is threatened by a shortage of the funds required for maintenance.

Not all the traditional symbols which create an image of the Netherlands in the far corners of the globe are enjoying a quiet retirement in the comfort of folklore. Some are still very much alive. For example, the bicycle, as any tourist trying to cross a road in Amsterdam will attest. Even the bicycle-addicted Chinese will reluctantly admit that the birthplace of the bicycle is in the Netherlands, but the reality is otherwise, as we have seen: the first bicycle was assembled by a British or French person, and the concept was fairly stolen by the Dutch. They do deserve the honour of having turned it into a commercial success, just as they have been exceptionally successful at stealing them.

At the heart of life we find the traditional Dutch symbol with the highest cuddle factor: the cow. They form an inseparable trio: the Dutchman, the grassy meadows and the national cuddly toy with the disarming expression, which is the cornerstone of the world-famous Dutch dairy industry. There are over four million cows in the Netherlands, including over 1.5 million dairy cows. However, the Dutchman was certainly not among the first to domesticate the ancestor of the cow, the aurochs. After all, the Dutchman's ancestor did not start farming until long after agriculture had already been developed comprehensively elsewhere.

The Dutch cow has, however, been a favourite export product for a very long time. A wooden board was found during the excavation of a Frisian *terp* which turned out to be a deed of sale from the first century. The occupant had flogged a cow to Roman soldiers who had been happy to hand over 115 *sestertii* and make the bike trip to the far north for the animal. The province of Friesland also played an important part in the development of the successful and hyper-modern Dutch cattle industry in later times. A statue of a cow was erected in Leeuwarden in honour of the Frisian pedigree cattle with the telling inscription, *Us Mem*, or Our Mother. Elsewhere in the country, too, there have been a number of statues dedicated to this indomitable symbol of prosperity, which also functions nicely as a lawnmower.

This reverence is understandable, as the Dutch cow is the world champion in milk production, and the breeding bulls' sperm also commands a decent price. The fact that the famous black and white figure is, in truth, hardly Dutch at all, is known only in professional circles. The Holstein-Friesian, as the brand-name goes, is an emigrant who came home. She is the descendant of cows which were sold to American farmers during the nineteenth century. About fifty years ago she made a triumphant comeback, as successful breeding methods had made her a better milk producer than her native colleague. Since then, she has seen golden times as the figurehead of Dutch cattle breeding and the traditional Dutch pastoral landscape.

Whether our bovine friends will continue to play this prominent role for much longer is open to question. Nowadays, almost twenty per cent of dairy cattle are permanently stalled and there is a good chance that in ten or so years the vast majority will only be seen indoors. The cause of this is the rapid drop in the number of dairy cattle businesses, which has led to upscaling and the disappearance of pasture around the remaining farms. In accordance with the tried and tested polder method, all those directly involved – the government, pressure groups and organisations promoting the protection of nature, animals and the environment – are looking in unison into ways of turning the tide. This has resulted so far in a project with the endearing title of *Koe & Wij* (Cow & Us), which is aimed at encouraging farmers to work together with them.

As far as the neighbours are concerned, they too want the cow to remain in the public domain for eternity. After all, the tourists who come in search of the traditional Dutch symbols sometimes cross the borders into their countries. They'd rather see the demise of another symbol: the coffeeshop, that accursed icon of Dutch liberality where youthful tourists sample the products of the hemp mills before returning home, in far too liberal a state of mind. The Dutch are able to laugh at such puritanical indignation. They have no fear of the liberal soft drugs policy being jeopardised, although the coffeeshops have little history of their own, especially compared to other traditional Dutch icons. Fifty or so years ago, soft drugs were hardly available, and for the nearest cannabis emporium you would have had to go to Afghanistan, which was a popular destination in those days. All the users from 'way back when' have to moan about these days are the, in their eyes, excessive prices and the fact that their favourite substances have disappeared from the menu: whatever happened to good old Red Lebanon, and how come you can't get hold of much good Afghan these days?

The most well-known Dutch symbol still in use and development has a considerably less controversial image: the famous tulip, which, in close cooperation with other colourful plants, has transformed the world's most famous clump of grass into a leading flower nation, a bulwark of flower power. The Dutch do all they can to maintain this reputation. They zealously fill their parks with flowers, and they will not rest until their gardens are an orgy of colour in spring and summer. Many consider their homes unfit for habitation unless there is at least one bouquet on the table. Furthermore, they make each other gifts of flowers at the drop of a hat, not just on the occasion of a birthday, party or dinner, but also 'just because'. Returning home from work, the Dutchman will frequently pick up a bunch for the missus – strangely enough, rarely for hubby, but at least in this way the Dutch can hang on to their urge for emancipation. The Dutch don't just say it with flowers, as the popular advertising slogan goes, they announce their message with clamorous cheer, they shout it from the rooftops and bellow it into each others' ears, continuously.

In doing so, they keep a flourishing floriculture industry afloat, from garden centres, florists and flower markets to gardeners, growers, auctions and exporters. Tens of thousands of people earn a living in this sector, which seems to have set itself the goal of turning the earth into a massive flowerbed. The Netherlands is the largest producer of cut flowers and plants and takes care of more than half of the global trade in these products. Each year, furthermore, about 6.5 billion bulbs are sent abroad. Can you imagine that? The export brings five million euros in for the world's biggest flower stall, annually. The beating heart of the business is two gigantic auctions: FloraHolland and Bloemenveiling Aalsmeer, which are about to merge, forming by far the largest floriculture auction in the world, which will not come as a surprise to anyone.

The Dutch abundance of flowers is used, down to the last grain of pollen, to promote the Netherlands as a colourful tourist destination, despite domestic grumblings about the 'corniness' of that image. The floriculture sector itself is also putting its best foot forward. Since 1985, Dutch 'flower arrangers' acting as missionaries for the floral image of the Netherlands have laid a large flower garden on Saint Peter's Square in Rome, where the Pope gives his traditional *Urbi et Orbi* address, every Easter. To finish, the Father of the Church turns to the flower men, equally traditionally, to utter the now-classic Dutch words in a thick German accent: *'Bedankt voor die bloemen'* ('Thank you for the flowers').

The intensive promotion is still effective. During the spring and summer, the tourists crowd around the splendour of the Keukenhof, the largest flower garden in the world. And, of course, around the famous bulb fields, which cover a tidy twenty-five thousand hectares. The multicoloured mosaics have caught people's imaginations before, according to the reports of eighteenth-century visitors. They were amazed at the scents, the constant stream of new breeds, which even then were widely exported, and the fact that every grower gave them a bouquet. To the dismay of the modern visitor to the fields, the flowers are beheaded before they reach full bloom, a barbaric custom that serves to strengthen the bulb.

Of all the plants which embellish the image of the Netherlands, the tulip is by far the most highly regarded. The plant, whose praises are sung in every way imaginable ('*Tulips from Amsterdam*'), is a solid national symbol, and moreover a symbol to be proud of – elegant, colourful and serene. And here is the rub: once again, the Dutch are strutting with borrowed plumage. The tulip is not a native plant at all, but was imported at the end of the sixteenth century from the Ottoman Empire, whose centre was what is now Turkey. Again the charitable judgement is that it was 'fairly stolen'. Even the word 'tulip' is an import: it is derived from the Turkish word *tulbend* (turban). It was not Turkey but Holland that went down in history as the land of the tulip due to the fact that the plant was brought to full flourish on Dutch soil, and became popular worldwide with its 'Product from the Netherlands' label.

First and foremost, the Dutch can thank the botanist Carolus Clusius for this. It was he who in 1593 planted the first tulip bulbs in the Hortus Botanicus of the University of Leiden. He also initiated the cultivation of tulips on the peat and polder lands behind the dunes which are still the heart of bulb culture. The cultivation quickly provided a variety of new species, which were adored in the seventeenth century as far away as Turkey.

The tulip became a craze in the Dutch Republic, especially among the upper middle class. They displayed a remarkable passion for beauty and collecting rare objects, and furthermore could afford their own gardens, where exotic species of plant were heartily welcomed. Gradually, the tulip became a status symbol, with a brisk trade in the provinces of Holland and Utrecht in particular. Demand quickly exceeded supply, causing prices to skyrocket, and ultimately astronomical sums were paid for bulbs which were still tucked away in the earth; a rare bulb would sometimes fetch as much as a nice Amsterdam canalside house. Speculators – known as 'florists' – did well out of what became known as 'tulipmania' and 'bulb madness'. The market collapsed in 1637 and thousands of tulip lovers were left destitute.

A typical feature of the enthusiasm that the tulip elicited were the special vases in which the wealthy aficionados exhibited their plants. These were not vases as we know them today, but real works of art with many different openings or spouts, each providing a flower with its own stage on which to shine in all its glory. These 'spouted vases' are seen as traditionally Dutch, but again – you know what's coming next – there's a catch. Similar vases had already been popular in the Middle East around the twelfth century. However, their popularity in wealthy European circles was first established in the Dutch Republic. The real *pièces de resistance* were produced in Delft in particular, and these found their way into countless foreign salons.

The town of Delft in the province of Zuid-Holland even became world-famous because of its 'Delft Blue', the white pottery with fine blue decoration which is still popular in the form of plates, bowls, tiles and miniature windmills. But no matter how popular and authentic it is, it was not invented in Delft: it is a not entirely successful – and therefore unintentionally original – imitation of Chinese porcelain, which the Dutch came across in the holds of captured Portuguese ships, and which was also imported by the Dutch East India Company. The delicate porcelain with its exotic blue decoration quickly became popular, so popular in fact that the domestic earthenware industry ran into problems. Although the raw materials and the procedure were unknown, a few manufacturers were able to roughly imitate the porcelain. As well as the Chinese motifs, they soon started using typically Dutch images as decoration, too.

Halfway through the seventeenth century, the Dutch conveniently took advantage of the downfall of the Chinese Ming dynasty, which dealt the Asiatic export trade a hefty blow. The pottery businesses shot up like mushrooms, particularly in Delft. In no time at all Delft Blue had taken over the world. You can still find old Delft Blue everywhere the Dutch traders set foot, sometimes in the form of impressive tile pictures. The many places which still attest to the high regard in which the earthenware was held include the palaces of Indian Maharajas and Tsar Peter the Great.

The famous, fragile pottery is still made by traditional methods; in Delft, of course, although similar earthenware with at least as good a reputation among experts comes from Gouda and Makkum (Friesland). Hand-painted vases, tiles, crockery and herring dishes are popular with big-spending tourists. Less well-off visitors are guaranteed to find something to their taste in the souvenir shops. However, if you are bent on purchasing genuine Delft Blue, caution is advised, as there is a good chance that the base of the so-authentic-looking blue-and-white vase is marked 'Made in China'. Strutting with borrowed plumage is no longer the exclusive province of the Dutch.

NO PLACe LiKE hOME

'Gezelligheid', the Dutch way

Every Dutch person knows exactly what *'gezelligheid'* is, but explaining the phenomenon to a foreigner is a different matter. *Gezelligheid* is considered the most difficult Dutch word to translate. Even so, it is constantly on the lips of the Dutch and the renowned *gezelligheid* is a cornerstone of Dutch culture. Without *gezelligheid*, the Dutch would be lost souls, condemned to muddle on eternally and meaninglessly.

Any foreigner who spends any length of time in the Netherlands is guaranteed to encounter *gezelligheid*, and should approach the phenomenon with an open mind. You see, it provides an excellent introduction to society. Join in with the *gezelligheid* and you will be a Dutchman among the Dutch. Whereas in the surrounding countries there's a strong chance an outsider will always remain an outsider, the threshold is lower in the Netherlands, although you may still stumble over it; *gezelligheid* is a game with unwritten, subtle rules.

This game is all about togetherness and security. Chatting, visiting each other, shopping together or dining out are all things which are *gezellig* or even *reuze gezellig* – 'very *gezellig*'. *Gezelligheid* is something you experience together, not alone. The *Homo neerlandicus* is known as a born individualist, but at the same time he is a social animal.

It takes some getting used to for the foreigner. In some cultures, people first meet on neutral territory and it is unusual to visit each other's houses. In the Netherlands, there is always the possibility that you will be invited into people's homes, even if you barely know them. 'Come round for a coffee some time,' is the standard invitation. It is a sentence that puzzles the uninitiated and can lead to the conversation taking an inadvertent turn:

'No, thanks, I don't like coffee. Did you know that coffee's bad for you, by the way?'

'Coffee? Black, or with milk?'

'But we can do that here, can't we? Look, there's a vending machine.'

You're not supposed to take the invitation literally. It is a courtesy ritual; a way of saying that you are welcome and the person would like to get to know you better. For those in the know, '*koffie drinken'* means 'we'll have a chat with a drink and perhaps some nibbles. It'll be *gezellig!*' If you'd rather have a glass of soya milk instead of coffee, that's fine too.

The idea is that you respond to the invitation with 'Oh, lovely, that sounds *gezellig!*' Unless of course you are not remotely interested in meeting up. If that's the case, it's worth knowing that the Dutch are masters of inventing excuses. They may be known for being candid, but declining unwanted invitations is an exception to the rule. If necessary, they will say they suddenly have to go to Vanuatu where a relative is in hospital following a botched performance during the world land-diving championships, the local variety of bungee jumping. Anything's better than having to utter the painful truth: 'Coffee? With *you*? Do me a favour, mate, I'd rather go land-diving in Vanuatu.'

Don't let it bother you if you don't understand the cryptic invitation, though. You will be forgiven. Steel yourself, though; it gets more cryptic, because once the initial misunderstanding has been overcome, the Dutchman will open his diary to see if he can 'find a gap' to 'schedule' the appointment. Seasoned ex-pats will also start leafing through their diaries, knowing that the consultation and consensus culture is sacred and that the Dutchman is a busy man in his leisure time. Apart from the family affairs common to most cultures – which in the Netherlands fall under the telling header of 'social obligations' – there are always plenty of other *gezellige* things going on. Moreover, the Dutch take very seriously the development of their children into all-round creatures of *gezelligheid* who are also capable of making individual choices in life. To this end, great distances are cycled on a weekly basis between clubs, courses, friends and school activities. The holy family culture also dictates that the evening meal is consumed at around six o'clock. Any visitor who turns up just before the sacred mealtime for a *gezellige* cup of coffee forms a major disruption to the lives of many Dutch people. This makes polder hospitality a complicated phenomenon. Foreigners who are unfamiliar with the finer details are flabbergasted at all the thumbing through diaries: is this the famed *gezelligheid*?

When the big day arrives, show that you are properly integrated by taking a bunch of flowers for the hostess. Don't overdo it – a big bunch of red roses is likely to cause consternation, particularly to the host – and be prepared for the lady of the house to say something odd: 'You shouldn't have done that!' All she means is 'How kind! Thank you, I'm flattered.'

It is also customary for the Dutch to shake hands when they meet on such occasions. In fact, they always do so, apart from when they see each other very often. They differ in this way from the French who, even in the workplace, cannot help themselves. For the Dutch, a vocal greeting will suffice, such as *'Hallo'*, *'Hé'* or *'Hai'*, although teenagers under the influence of the refined MTV culture are more likely to use 'Whazzup?' or the more personal 'Yo, *lekker ding!*' ('Yo, hot stuff!').

People rarely kiss on a first meeting, but this is more than made up for later on. For a long time it was common for friends and relatives to kiss each other once on each cheek, but for some inexplicable reason these days it takes three kisses to make things *gezellig*. The nation awaits the continued development of the ritual with baited breath. In order to avoid misunderstandings, it's worth remembering that men rarely kiss each other. Even in the easygoing Netherlands this still comes with a certain shame attached.

Once the threshold has been crossed, you have penetrated the inner sanctum of Dutch *gezelligheid*. The Dutch do all they can to make their homes *gezellig*, so that its occupants feel secure in them. And, one has to admit, many Dutch living rooms are extremely pleasant. This cherished homeliness is expressed in old-fashioned Dutch sayings such as *'Oost west, thuis best'*, *'Eigen haard is goud waard'* and *'Zoals het klokje thuis tikt, tikt het nergens'*, which all amount to much the same as 'No place like home'. Such maxims, engraved on little tiles, adorned the walls of many a living room until not so long ago. These tiles also bore profound nuggets of wisdom such as the brilliant 'Nobody has a programme for the concert of life', but most seem to have ended up in boxes in attics.

One reason for this Dutch homeliness is the changeable climate, though it seems that the deep-seated urge to keep the country, densely-populated and hard-won from the sea, habitable has a part in it – people in countries with similar climates often pay much less attention to the décor of their homes. The still-cherished bourgeois ideal of order and tidiness can also be traced back to this. Lots of houses are paragons of decency. In centuries gone by, foreigners were often impressed by the diligence with which the Dutch took care of their living environment. According to some, this hardworking, neat people even scrubbed the pavements with milk.

Whether or not the image of tidily-kept public spaces was ever correct, such spaces are now hopelessly soiled with litter. The Dutch are happy to leave the maintenance of the public domain to the relevant authorities, and they don't throw any milk at all on the street; at best, the empty package. Separated waste collection, however, has been a great success in the Netherlands, and there are plenty of initiatives, mostly by local authorities, aimed at keeping the environment clean and 'green'. With slogans on litter bins such as 'Keep the neighbourhood clean', the wall tile has made inroads into public spaces.

However, behind closed doors, the Dutchman will do all he can to keep his paradise tidy, and he doesn't mind showing it. To the amazement of many foreigners, he often leaves the curtains open at night, as if to say 'Look how fantastic it is for us here!' Even so, the home is not a museum in which every fingerprint is taboo and visitors are prohibited from touching anything. The Dutch are usually informal and hospitable. The head of the family welcomes guests with a cordial 'Make yourself at home'. However, this hospitality has clear limits: visitors are not expected to bluntly put their feet up on the table, eat all the biscuits or help themselves to beer from the fridge.

In the past, the dining table was the heart of the home. A well-used cliché was that after dinner the whole family would sit *gezellig* around the table, playing traditional Dutch games under the light of a single lamp under the watchful gaze of the wall tiles. And if the *gezelligheid* was sufficient, it could run on late. '*Gezelligheid* knows no time' as another classic tile wisdom went.

But the games have made way for the television, which is put to great use in the land of the electronics pioneer, Philips, often in several rooms at once. And not without reason as the roughly ten Dutch TV channels are a great source of *gezelligheid* and amusement. It is no mere coincidence that the world-famous *Big Brother*, the mother of all *reality*-shows, is a Dutch invention. In the programme's wake, all channels started putting the 'regular Dutch person' on the stage. Since then they have been plastered wall-to-wall with 'reality' and 'emo' TV and regular Dutch persons have been lining up to share their own squalor with the masses. They lament lost loves, broken familial bonds and leaking roofs, try to get to Beijing as quickly as possible while tripping over shoelaces, snack on delicious deep-fried crickets with endangered African tribes and allow themselves to be locked up in big houses by the dozen, as if it were nothing. Once there they gossip and provoke each other to breaking point, vomit over each other, sneakily do 'it' together and get up to many more *gezellige* antics.

It's all one big party, especially as simultaneously on three other channels the *BNer* is performing his or her tricks. The abbreviation 'BN' stands for *Bekende Nederlander* (Famous Dutch person) not 'banal', as I had initially feared. *BNers* are perhaps the most *gezellige* of all the Dutch: night after night, all-singing, all-cooking and all-ice-dancing, they provide us with entertainment, while on another channel fellow *BNers* interrogate them about their school years, their new cars, their recent divorces and the problems of ice-dancing – in short, everything that matters to the world at large. It's also marvellous to see how their numbers multiply: once a 'regular Dutch person' has allowed himself to be locked up in a house, it's only a matter of time before he's dancing on ice too. Before too long, the entire population will be *BNers*. It's an apt development for a society which in many respects is the most classless in the world.

With such a rich variety of *gezelligheid*, it's no wonder that the massive commercial breaks during and in between programmes are now filled with advertisements for TV sets for the kitchen. After all, you may miss a soap opera or a football match, or, worse still, an hour-long live broadcast explaining how an obscure member of the royal family has cut himself shaving or that the queen has given birth to her forty-ninth grandchild. At the same time, lovers of in-depth documentaries and news programmes are well-catered for: thanks to the wide-ranging cable network a large number of Belgian, British and German channels have long been available. Those in the handful of one-horse towns where cable is not available have satellite dishes to fall back on. By the way, the satellite dish has also gained remarkable ground in the big cities. For many immigrants from the Mediterranean region, it forms an umbilical cord to the homeland, and many older urban districts are known as 'satellite cities' of Ankara or Rabat.

As well as a decent TV set, the normal Dutch living room also contains central heating radiators, along with an open fireplace for the sake of *gezelligheid*, and a large number of plants, at least one bouquet of flowers and sometimes amazingly versatile wall decorations. If at all possible, the Dutch will have some 'art on the wall', home-made if necessary. Even back in the seventeenth century, foreign visitors noted in astonishment that an unusual number of Dutch living rooms, even in farmhouses, contained oil paintings, a luxury that was more or less unheard-of elsewhere.

The interior design is generally according to individual taste, although many homes do remind one strongly of small museums. Collecting seems to be a national passion. In many cases, this is initially down to coincidence. You buy a pretty porcelain deer to go on the windowsill and by coincidence receive another as a gift. 'Now you've got a collection,' is what people tend to say. This is the start of an impassioned scraping together of a thousand little deer. Many a terraced house is bursting at the seams with such knick-knacks. The hobby develops into a lifetime fulfilment: contacts are made, trips are undertaken and fairs are visited. The *Verzame-laarsjaarbeurs* in Utrecht is the largest collectors' fair in Europe.

Trips like this are not only practical, they are also extremely *gezellig*. The Dutch have long been used to seeking *gezelligheid* outside the home. The café is a traditional source of *gezelligheid*, and particularly the homely 'brown pub', which derives its name from the wooden furniture and panelling. There you can enjoy yourself in the company of friends and the rapidly-growing number of singles can meet for a chat or a game of cards or billiards. The nostalgic notion of the 'local' is being eroded, however. A common complaint is that most places of entertainment are becoming dominated by prosperous young people who like to 'go wild' in boisterous fashion. These moans certainly hold water with regard to discos, but luckily there are still plenty of cafés which don't instantly remind one of the school canteen.

Because of the growing prosperity in recent decades, the homeliness has ventured outside the home into other areas of social life. The countless pavement cafés which are filled as soon as the sun shows its face are testimony to this, as is the proliferation of holiday parks. Increasingly, the Dutch like to head off for a couple of days with family and friends and the 'bungalow' is by far the favourite destination. There you can make your own coffee and even use your own placemats and tablecloth. Proportionally, no other country has as many holiday parks as the Netherlands.

Neither is there any other country where club life is as buoyant as in the polders. It's hard to think of a theme that is not represented by at least one association, which of course holds meetings intensively. The same type of solidarity still exists in some neighbourhoods. Although 'the neighbourhood' has suffered severely throughout the western world as a binding element, street parties are still regular fixtures in some places. The national 'children's play day' is also used in some areas as a way of strengthening ties within districts. The same effect is intended with the national 'neighbours day', a brand new phenomenon instigated by the Netherlands' best-known coffee producer, whose profits are boosted by every new form of *gezelligheid*.

A favourite topic of conversation among male residents during such events is the recent renovation of the house, garage, shed or garden. Building, painting and decorating are never-ending activities in many Dutch homes – the *gezelligheid* is never finished, and things can always be made more *gezellig*, homely and cosy. Renovation is a national hobby and the do-it-yourself (DIY) centres do very well out of it. Tens of thousands of families set off on Boxing Days and Easter Mondays for one of the many *woonboulevards* (furniture malls) which open their doors specially.

And if there's really nothing left to plaster or partition, the DIY enthusiast turns his attention to outside: isn't it time for a new bench in the garden? A picnic table under a pergola draped in grapevines, for example, surrounded by old-fashioned lanterns and overlooking a nice little pond with Japanese koi? Of course, you know full well that before long it will be emptied by a heron, but it is *gezellig* after all. And anyway, it's quite nice to have a heron in the garden. Before you know it, the garden will be a scene of havoc for weeks on end.

All this violence has put the traditional resident of Dutch gardens on a defensive footing: the garden gnome has become a threatened species. The Garden Gnome Liberation Front – an anonymous group which fights for the rights of the 'oppressed and exploited' gnome – is partly responsible for this. Gnomes are often 'liberated' and released into the wild. Recently, the residents of an old people's home discovered that several dozen gnomes had been set loose in their large garden. The senior citizens were concerned about the poor little fellows and all were given scarves to repel the winter cold. One such resident, who for understandable reasons prefers to remain anonymous, spoke to a local newspaper of the 'humanitarian mission' as the only suitable solution to this 'violation of human rights'. Over the next few days, neighbours brought along even more displaced gnomes who were also generously granted asylum in the garden of the home.

There are yet more victims of the unrelenting pond of *gezelligheid*. The jigsawed goose which for years adorned thousands of windowsills has become an endangered species, too. The modern Dutchman prefers a roof tile next to the front door bearing the family name, or the word *Welkom* in decoartive lettering. The ancient custom of naming the house is also under great pressure. Carved maxims such as *'Oost west, thuis best'*, *'Waarheen leidt de weg?'* ('Where does the road lead to?') and – somewhat less *gezellig* – *'Het Vagevuur'* ('Purgatory') have also gone the way of the wall tiles.

My parental home appeared to bear the name *Gunda* when it was purchased, in decorative shadowed lettering on a rustic wooden plate attached to the facade. This unusual word sounded to me like the name of the hero of a Scandinavian saga, but turned out to be an abbreviation of the tackiest sort: *Gezellige Uurtjes Na Dagelijkse Arbeid* (*Gezellige* hours after daily labour). Nevertheless, I thought the sign was a beauty, and my protests were heard from afar when my father unceremoniously sawed it into pieces and threw it into the wood burner.

However, one occupant of the home has weathered all storms thus far: the pet. Millions of cats and dogs knock about the Dutch living room, along with a herd of rabbits, hamsters, guinea pigs, marmots and feathered friends that would make Noah blush. *'Gezellig!'* say the Dutch, who see the cuddly housemates as a source of homeliness and distraction. For foreigners, though, the presence of pets is sometimes a nuisance, particularly when the dog of the house starts to mount a leg clad in Sunday best. Many cultures hold that beasts do not belong in the home, and in civilised countries they shouldn't be seen on the street either.

'Welcome in the country of dogshit' is the first thing my friend from Singapore always says when I meet him at the airport. His distaste for what he calls 'pet fetishism' is as sincere as it is heartfelt. Similarly, few Dutch people find it *gezellig* that next-door's dog answers the call of nature on their pavement. In order to combat such inconvenience a number of local authorities have introduced *hondenuitlaatveldjes* where dogs can be let off the lead, followed by fenced-off areas of parkland which have been christened 'dog toilets'. These initiatives haven't really helped.

However, the greatest culture shock encountered by foreign visitors is the Dutch toilet. The Dutch view their restrooms – known in the vernacular as 'the smallest room' – not as a necessary annex to the home but as a part of the home which is also entitled to some *gezelligheid*. At the very least, you should give it a proper lick of paint or paper the walls, and hang up a mirror or a birthday calendar. It's just as common, however, to find the toilet decorated with posters, a couple of plants and a stack of magazines and books, for which a special cabinet has been installed in many cases. The finishing touch is provided by toilet paper printed with comical pictures. Foreign guests often spend some time admiring what in their eyes is a crazy spectacle, and in turn elicit surprise from the host or hostess, who may be sufficiently concerned to ask what has come over the guest.

The astonishment at this deranged decorative frenzy pales into insignificance, however, next to the horror that the toilet user is faced with at the sight of the Dutch toilet bowl, with its unique shelf. What dark forces must have consumed a people who see fit to adorn its toilets with a stage for its own bowel movements? How intensely filthy must the collective trauma be to manifest itself in such an extreme form of self-chastisement?

The standard explanations for this fine specimen of Dutch design make no impression whatsoever on the despairing house guest. The toilet user's buttocks are spared from splashing? Well, yes, that *is* important! A clever invention so that one can study the stools of poorly children? Haven't you people heard of hospitals?

The disbelief has given rise to a range of groundbreaking theories around the Dutch instrument of torture they call the toilet bowl. According to some, it has originated from the deep-seated Dutch mania for ordering and keeping everything. Others are convinced that it has to do with the ingrained penchant for water management. 'There's no doubt about it,' an American who has lived in the Netherlands for years confided in me, 'I know the Dutch. If they can't see land protruding above water, they are inconsolable.'

It's no wonder, then, that the toilet often plays a central role in the reports of journalists and writers on their adventures in the hospitable Netherlands – adventures which are often overshadowed by obstinate cases of constipation.

GeT YoUR PARtY hAT oN AnD GEt GOïNG!

Merrymaking without meaning

Foreigners who wish to learn about the Netherlands cannot reasonably avoid the national holidays. After all, these holidays are the icing on the cake of national culture. In a country like the Netherlands in particular, where that cake consists of a large number of layers of such a variety of tastes and colours, it's instructive to see which events have become truly unifying to the nation as a whole and how these festivities are celebrated.

Of course, visitors do not have to be Sherlock Holmes to be able to form a decent idea of this. Indeed, the Dutch are known to all for being cool customers who are austere and restrained. Furthermore, many foreigners know by heart *Hans Brinker or The Silver Skates*, the classic bestseller in which the Dutchman is laid bare in all his traditional peculiarity. On the basis of this reliable information, it's clear the Dutch celebrate in an extremely subdued fashion. They gather in the prettiest farmhouse in the locality, sitting in two opposing rows – women on the left, men on the right – in an overlit best room with a pastry on each lap and a glass of *advocaat* (eggnog) within arm's reach, on an oak stool with a small Persian rug on it. One of the men will some-times speak quietly to his neighbour, who will nod knowingly, but otherwise the company will sit shrouded in stoical silence. Until ten past nine, when Uncle Evert cracks a joke, at which point the partygoers get boisterously stuck into half a glass of beer. By ten o'clock, the group has been loaded into three Honda Civics and then lurches home. Along the way, Uncle Evert sticks his head out of a half-opened window and shouts at the top of his voice, to the hilarity of all, *'Oranje Boven!'* ('Orange on top!') The last farmhouse turns its lights out by around half past ten, and life returns to normality the next day.

If you've imagined the parties to be like this, you really do need to visit the Netherlands. You won't see much of this con-straint, particularly during public holidays. Such occasions are ideal opportunities to see the austere Dutch really letting their hair down.

The most popular of these holidays is *Koninginnedag*, in honour of the birthday of Queen Beatrix. The monarch's actual birthday is on the 31st of January, but as the Dutch winter is less than ideal for a national party, she decided on her coronation in 1980 that the birthday of her popular mother, Juliana, would continue to be used: April 30th. The Netherlands is probably the only country where the royal birthday is not actually celebrated on the day itself.

Most Dutch people are not fervent monarchists at all, but despite this they are not going to pass up on the opportunity for a good old knees-up. Especially if the fun is accompanied by another beloved characteristic of the Dutch: bartering. In countless homes in the days preceding Koninginnedag, the often-crammed attic is emptied. On the day itself, tens of thousands of Dutch people set off early in the morning for the ubiquitous fleamarkets, in a colourful parade of overloaded bicycles, bulging shopping trolleys and old prams. The result of the general habit of keeping 'old junk' is literally on the streets for all to see. If it doesn't sell, you simply take it back home: Koninginnedag will come around again next year. Ardent collectors are also up and about at the crack of dawn: who knows, they might find the porcelain deer they need to complete their collection.

The rest of the country also takes to the streets in the course of the day, dressed in the national colour of orange. Riding waves of alcohol, music and deep-fryer fumes, they stroll from stall to pavement café in high spirits. In many places, the party concludes with a spectacular fireworks display, although some ragged partygoers can be found wandering the streets until late in the night, looking for the way home.

By this point, the birthday girl herself has long returned home. During the day, according to tradition, the Queen visits two towns in which she is treated to demonstrations of clog-making, herring-gutting, 'biting-the-cake', sack racing and other traditional

Dutch folklore activities. The sovereign puts her best foot forward. She shakes the hands of hundreds of children and has a smile and a friendly word for everyone. Beatrix has the reputation of being somewhat standoffish, but also serious and committed.

The successor to the throne, Crown Prince Willem-Alexander, is usually also in attendance. He is somewhat more jovial and is closer to the people than his mother, especially since his marriage to the extrovert Argentinean Máxima Zorreguieta. He has turned out to be a sports fan who exuberantly celebrates Dutch sporting victories. This has given him the unflattering nickname of 'Prins Pils'. Now older and wiser, he has set the record straight by becoming a member of the International Olympic Committee. Furthermore, he has dedicated himself to a traditional Dutch specialisation: water management. His chairmanship of the United Nations' Advisory Board on Water and Sanitation has meant his old nickname has been banished for good: 'Prins Pils' is now 'Prins Water'.

The bond between the House of Oranje and the Netherlands is a strong one, and is aptly described as a marriage. A marriage that has stood strong for centuries, as both have histories which are closely intertwined. The Oranje dynasty was even present at the cradle of Dutch independence, although its roots are not on the North Sea coast but in the medieval county of Nassau, in what is now Germany. The Nassaus acquired sizeable territories in the Low Countries through strategic marriages, which was a common method of expanding power at the time. The southern French principality of Orange – which probably derives its name from the flourishing trade in oranges – also fell into their hands in this way. This is how the title of *Prins van Oranje* (Prince of Orange), along with the territories of the Nassaus in the Low

Countries, came into the hands of one Willem I van Nassau, nicknamed 'the Silent', during the mid-sixteenth century.

Willem van Oranje went on to become the leader of the resistance to the Spanish rule which burdened the Netherlands. The reason for this conflict was the infringement of old privileges and the merciless persecution of lowlands Calvinists by the Catholic King of Spain. Due to a strange confluence of circumstances, the Revolt resulted at the end of the sixteenth century in the birth of the independent Republic of the Seven United Netherlands, the predecessor of the modern Netherlands. Willem himself never saw this, as he was murdered in his Delft home on July 10th 1584. Here, in what is now the Prinsenhof Museum, two bullet holes in the wall are a memorial to the man who has gone down in history as the 'Father of the Fatherland'. The fact that the holes were made later on does not detract from the importance of the place where 'the Silent', according to the chronicles, spoke his final historic words – not in Dutch, but in the French common in courtly circles at the time: 'My God, have pity on me and this poor people.' There was to be no such pity for the assassin, whose severed head adorned the city walls of Delft for a while.

The Dutch owe their royal house and its most important national symbols to Willem and his Revolt: the flag and the national anthem, named after the Prince. The *Wilhelmus* is renowned as the oldest and most unusual national anthem in the world, although it was not chosen as the national hymn until 1932. The lyrics, written by the Prince's allies around 1570, are not a tribute to the virtues and glory of the fatherland, as most anthems are, but a lengthy monologue by Willem. In it he explains that as a devout Christian, he has loyally served the Spanish king, but the king's tyranny has given him just reason to revolt. A 'Father of the Fatherland' who gives account of his rebellion against the competent authorities: it is unique among national anthems.

The Dutch flag is also a reminder of the Revolt. The red, white and blue was first hoisted by the rebels, although the uppermost bar was orange, in honour of Willem van Oranje: this is the origin of the famous cry of *Oranje Boven!* Blue was the colour of the line of Nassau. When the House of Oranje was driven out of the Republic during the French Period (1795-1814), the orange in the *'Prinsenvlag'* made way for red. The red remained in place after the return of the House of Oranje in 1815, this time as true sovereigns of a brand-new constitutional monarchy, but the colour was squabbled over until well into the last century: should it be red or orange? It finally remained red, but by way of compromise, an orange pennant is attached to the top of the flagpole on Koninginnedag and the birthdays of the crown prince and his wife and children.

Even so, the old prince's flag is still flown. Not in the Netherlands but on the other side of the Atlantic Ocean, on the facade of New York's City Hall. The official flag of the metropolis differs from the old princely bunting on two points only: the orange, white and blue are displayed vertically and the white bar bears the city arms. This includes four windmill sails, flanked by a seventeenth-century Dutch colonist and an Indian from the island of Manahatta (Manhattan). Below the seal is the number 1625, the year in which the Dutch bought the island from the Indians and founded New Amsterdam, the city that was to become New York. The flag is one of the tangible reminders of the historical influence of the Dutch on North American society.

On Koninginnedag, the Netherlands is a sea of red, white and blue, and the Dutch sing their national anthem with relish. That is, they sing the first couple of lines, as no one knows all fifteen verses. Neither does your average Dutchman have the slightest idea what he is singing. The confusion sets in by the second line – '*Ben ik van Duitsen bloed*' ('I am of German blood'). German blood? Me?! Get lost! By the seventh line – '*De Koning van Spanje heb ik altijd geëerd*' ('I have always honoured the King of Spain') – he has completely lost his way. Honour the King of Spain? Not on your life! What kind of a lunatic song is this?

The meaning of the flag and the national coat of arms – another symbol of the close ties between the Oranjes and the nation – is also only known to a few. If you say so, thinks the reveller; his motto is 'Get your party hat on and get going'.

National consciousness in the Netherlands is not particularly well-developed, to put it mildly. To most Dutch people, being Dutch is mainly practical in meaning: Dutch is what you are because that's what your passport says. Strong national sentiments are rare and are expressed primarily during major football and skating events. The scarceness of national symbols on the street speaks volumes: exuberant flag-waving is reserved for holidays, and other formal symbols are hard to find. The tulip has made a greater impression than the image of Her Majesty. Dutch people who refuse to buy stamps bearing her image on principle are no exception.

In fact, many Dutch people boast of the fact that they completely lack any sense of national consciousness, and that this is what distinguishes the Dutch from less civilised peoples. Although this view is brimming with inherent contradictions, foreigners would be wise not to dispute this sensitive point with the Dutch.

The oversensitivity concerning terms such as 'national consciousness' and 'national identity' dates largely from the second half of the last century. The first post-war generation in particular held a magnifying glass to anything that might refer to it in any way: could this perhaps pave the way for the dreaded nationalism? This reflex arose from the horrors of the Second World War, and in particular the Holocaust, which had a devastating effect on the large Jewish community of the Netherlands. Making the concept of national identity taboo left its mark on history teaching: the old-fashioned 'learning of facts by heart' faded into the background and the emphasis was placed fully on the 'lessons of the Second World War'. 'The history of the fatherland' became a tainted expression.

Apart from incidental outpourings, the lack of a hallowed national identity was never even a point, much less a problem. How important was it that citizens should know the meaning behind their national holidays? Did it make these holidays any less enjoyable? Did anyone lose sleep over it?

However, at the start of this century, the harmonious unity turned suddenly into apprehension. To the nation's shock, the realisation dawned that the knowledge of national history and culture was poor across the board. It wouldn't be too long before the Dutch mistook the naval hero Michiel de Ruyter for the inventor of the chocolate sprinkles of the same name.

The government resolved to deal with the problem by restoring the previously neglected factual knowledge. It set up a commission to establish a 'historical canon': a historical infusion that history teachers could give their students comprising fifty incontrovertible milestones in the birth of the Netherlands. The commission's explanation demonstrated the impact the struggle with national identity also had on them. It stated that the canon was not intended as a 'vehicle for national pride' but as a way of encouraging 'involvement' in Dutch history.

Of course, any canon is going to be somewhat random in character and the Dutch were quick to point out missing themes to the commission. Whole professional groups rose up and decided to create their own canons. Regions also claimed their own canons. The consequence of this was that the whole country fell under the spell of the canon: canons rained down from all corners of Dutch culture.

Before long, the Dutchman will be a walking encyclopaedia of Dutch history and culture, capable of answering any question regarding its public holidays. However, even now there is plenty of reason for the curious foreigner to immerse himself in the festive buzz. You see, how the Dutch celebrate is equally as telling as the answer to the question of what they celebrate. Parties in domestic circles in particular offer ideal opportunities for getting to know the much-praised Dutch *gezelligheid*.

The interested foreigner who wishes to study the core culture of the Dutch from top to bottom should try ringing random doorbells dressed as a bishop on the evening of December 5th. Then, the whole country is in the thrall of the number one family occasion, *Sint-Nicolaas*, and what better way is there to infiltrate this traditional Dutch feast than as the lead player himself?

The festivities revolve around gifts which are distributed in the name of Saint Nicholas, popularly known as *Sinterklaas*. The elderly saintly gent is a bit of an odd-looking character – he tends to stand out with his long white beard, loose red cape, mitre and staff – but he is well known as a true friend of children. Young children are absolutely convinced of his existence and eagerly await his arrival from distant Spain every year, where, according to folklore, he lives. He arrives around November 20th in a ramshackle steamboat with his trusty grey steed and pitch-black helpers (*Zwarte Pieten* or Black Peters) at dozens of ports simultaneously. In the ensuing weeks he follows an intensive itinerary around department stores, clubhouses and staff associations. Everywhere he goes he is greeted with the full repertoire of melodious Sinterklaas songs – and every Dutch person does actually know the words to these – and hands out gifts while the exotically-clad Peters dish out spice nuts as if their lives depend on it.

If they are lucky, children are allowed to 'put a shoe out' a few times during the preceding weeks. Before they go to bed they leave a shoe next to the heater containing a carrot or some hay for the Sint's horse. According to tradition, the saint rides over the rooftops at night and has his helpers throw gifts down the chimneys into the shoes – a somewhat laborious and risky method of delivery, for which anyone else would need at least one permit. The fact that many modern homes don't have chimneys has not deterred a single child, and neither does the fact that there seem to be quite a few Sints at any one time on the prettily-illuminated streets cause much consternation. When I was a boy, a good fifty of them left the home of my neighbour, who worked as a make-up artist, on December 5th, but as long as every Peter gave me a handful of spice nuts I didn't ask any awkward questions.

Excited children eagerly await the outcome of *pakjesavond* (the evening when gifts are given), as the Sint is good to nice children but strict on naughty ones. Those who have often misbehaved even run the risk of ending up in the jute sack in which Sinterklaas carries the presents. Their lot is an inglorious and giftless trip to Spain. The fact that this never actually happens is a secret that adults and older children guard with exemplary discipline. No wonder, as they are also treated on Sinterklaas night.

They mercilessly rib each other with imaginative 'surprises', often accompanied by hilarious verses. In these, they often tell each other a few home truths in the name of the saintly one. Loved ones, relatives, bosses and other superiors: no one escapes the typical Sinterklaas mockery, which they'd never get away with at any other time of the year.

Just about everyone agrees that the ritual-charged Sinterklaas feast is one of the nicest Dutch traditions. For a while it looked as if the Sint would be ousted by Santa Claus, the jolly do-gooder from the North Pole who, in North America, was cloned from the Sinterklaas introduced by Dutch colonists from whom his name is derived. Thankfully, the Dutch unmasked him as a third-rate imitator just in time, despite his Dutch roots.

It seems remarkable that the good saint's holiday is seen as an authentic piece of Dutch folklore, as after all, what is a bishop who lived in the Byzantine city of Myra around the year 300 doing in the Netherlands, and in the company of a group of oddly-dressed blacked-up white people? And how did this 'fighting bishop', who landed in prison during the Council of Nicaea in the year 325 after laying out a colleague with a well-aimed fist, become a friend of the children? It will probably come as no surprise to you that few Dutch people can answer these questions.

There is no doubt that the bishop led a colourful existence, but after his death it became considerably more so. Posthumously, Nicholas became a worker of miracles, and some of the miracles attributed to him are the basis for his reputation as a generous uncle to all children. Because of other miracles he was also made the patron saint of sailors, which made him highly popular in countless port cities. One church after another was erected in his name and in Amsterdam, he actually became the patron of the entire city. However, Nicholas demonstrated an unusual versatility: he also became the patron saint of merchants, bankers, bakers, butchers, prostitutes, thieves and prisoners.

His European career only reached full fruition after 1087 when Italian merchants stole his bones from Myra, in what is now Turkey. Since then he has laid in Bari, where his real triumphal parade began. He was the most popular of the saints in large areas of Europe during the late Middle Ages. At the time the Italian port was under Spanish rule, and furthermore, Spain was seen as the cradle of all that was beautiful and exotic. Black Peter was also linked to Spain: he was said to be descended from the Moors, although the Italians claim him as a representative of the renowned chimneysweep's guild. Others believe he was originally the personification of the devil, who Nicholas triumphed over. The celebration of Sint-Nicolaas originally took place on December 6th, the saint's name day. *Pakjesavond* was later moved to December 5th in the Netherlands.

During the Reformation, everything possible was done to ensure the demise of the Nicholas cult, but this met little success in the officially Calvinist Dutch republic with its extensive underground Catholic minority. The Saint was embraced into the bosom of the Dutch family and the cultural cross-pollination proudly stood firm. With the aid of an enthusiastic middle class, his position became even stronger in later centuries.

The Sinterklaas party can rightly be considered the icing on the cake of the national culture. However, the most popular family occasion is not actually an official holiday. This honour is reserved for Koninginnedag, New Year's Day and a full seven Christian holidays. The abundance of Christian feast days has often surprised foreigners. For instance, Easter, Whitsun and Christmas are celebrated on two days and there's also an official holiday on Ascension Day. On these days shops are normally closed.

This abundance is plainly excessive in such a highly secular-ised society, where 'somethingism' is the main religious move-ment. Especially when you consider that the approximately one million Muslims do not have a single national holiday. The suggestion has been put forward to scrap one of the Christian holidays from the calendar in favour of Idd al-Fitr – the Islamic celebration at the end of Ramadan – but this has slipped from the agenda without a murmur. Similarly, proposals to turn the Hindu 'festival of light', Diwali, or the anniversary of the abolition of slavery into a national holiday came to nothing.

Dutch people of foreign origin party on regardless and some of these festivities even have a national feel. The *Pasar Malam Besar* (Great Evening Market) in The Hague is not solely for those Dutch people with links to the former colony of the Dutch East Indies, but for large sections of the population an annual festive outing. The South American-style Tropical Summer Carnival in Rotterdam also draws hundreds of thousands of visitors every year. This originally Antillean festival has developed into a grand multicultural spectacle. Just like the 'normal' carnival celebrated mainly in the originally Catholic southern provinces of Brabant and Limburg, these festivals hold great meaning for many but have no official status. This doesn't trouble many Dutch people, but in comparison with the dominant Christian festivity on the official holiday calendar, it is a quirky fact.

However, the most remarkable aspect of this calendar is still the lack of a celebration of true national importance. You could view Koninginnedag as such, of course, and the same applies to Liberation Day. The celebration of the German surrender on May

5th 1945, ending the Second World War in the Netherlands, is the only public holiday that bears comparison with Koninginnedag in terms of size and exuberance. This cheerfulness is inseparable from the austerity with which the Dutch remember their dead on the preceding evening, but Liberation Day is only an official holiday once every five years, and the only official aspect of Remembrance is the ceremony, broadcast on TV and radio, around the national 'two minutes' silence' including the laying of the royal wreath in Amsterdam.

The list of official holidays includes no remembrance of the Revolt against Spanish rule, for example, the assassination of the 'Father of the Fatherland' or the formation of the united Dutch state – events which would be printed in capitals on other countries' festive calendars. It is characteristic for a nation which has never been concerned much with national identity and national consciousness, and even prides itself on this fact.

'ARE YoU TrYING to POISON ME?'

In praise of Dutch cuisine

'It's a good thing they widened the doorway during renovations,' a foreign correspondent once wrote after visiting a well-known Dutch restaurant, 'At least we were able to get out quickly.' And neither was an Australian who had lived in the Netherlands for years taken with what he had been given to eat in the country. In his book about the period, he put the whole of Dutch cuisine on his 'vomit list'.

What's happening to the image of our national food culture? Why is Dutch food such an inexhaustible source of disapproval and mockery? Those two negative comments are certainly not unique. In the eyes of many a foreigner, the Netherlands is a culinary desert. They just mash everything to a pulp there in the polders. They eat raw fish and other dishes from the early stages of civilisation. Quasi-respectably, they hold their olfactory organs, mutated by years of exposure to sickly pancakes, over glasses of wine in restaurants not worthy of the name. They gnaw away at a mysterious smoked sausage speciality called *rockworst*, as was discovered by a popular British travel guide which rates itself as the 'most authoritative guide in the field of travel'.

Is it really that bad? There's no accounting for taste, but a lot of the criticism is, to use a culinary term, baloney. The Australian presents such dishes as rabbit curry, fish pudding, potatoes with sugar and other phantom fare as typical Dutch dishes. And not so long ago a major German magazine wrote that all Dutch people were crazy about *balkenbrij*, a traditional dish of meat scraps, blood and fat that most Dutch people have never even seen, let alone eaten. It seems that if you don't exaggerate the native eating habits in a grotesque fashion, you are clearly no expert on the Netherlands.

It's as if there wasn't already enough for the writers to sneer at. Without exception, they profess their disdain for the lamentable frugality which, in their eyes, is so typical of the pit of culinary despair that is the Netherlands. The *stamppotten* (a type of stew) in particular come in for a slating: kale with *rockworst*, sauerkraut with *rockworst*, even a main course soup with *rockworst* – without exception, the nourishing Dutch cuisine is an insult to the taste buds.

To the horror of all and sundry, even if *stamppot* is not on the menu the Dutch will demonstrate that they are high priests of the mashing culture. Whatever adorns their plates, it will be mixed and mashed without mercy. Some Hollandologists claim to detect a salient similarity between this barbaric habit and the polder model: according to such experts, the Dutch consensus culture also invariably provides a characterless compromise once all the opinions have been mashed together.

Even the popular pancake, the filling delicacy which has brought up whole generations of tough dike guardians, is seen as an excellent example of the formidable mashing of the polders. Anything that is in any way digestible is thrown into the batter: raisins, bacon, apple, you name it. And, while you're at it, douse it in another dollop of sugar and syrup.

And the never-ending stream of potatoes! There are foreigners who believe that the vegetable was developed in the laboratory of a malevolent Dutch geneticist called Eigenheimer. Perhaps this idea was inspired by Vincent van Gogh's famous painting, *The Potato Eaters*. At any rate, it has encouraged the idea that all Dutch people are peasants with potato-like faces, who live in Hansel-and-Gretel houses and jab joylessly away at spuds until late at night.

However, the pinnacle of disgust is the Dutchman's age-old love of the herring. What has possessed a fairly modern nation to elevate a raw fish to the status of delicacy? And not only that, but to consume it in broad daylight, in full view of unsuspecting tourists? Surely it's now time to set up special herring zones, far from built-up areas, for the malodorous herring stalls, those popular hang-out places where an endless supply of fish is cut into ribbons, served up with a sprinkling of raw onion and eaten off a rectangular cardboard plate? Preferably, one uses a cocktail stick with a *gezellige* Dutch flag on it, to lend the ritual not only a national flavour but also a certain innocence and homeliness. And surely, isn't it time we brought to an end the macabre custom of *haringhijsen* (herring hoisting), popular in Rotterdam and the surrounding areas, the sinister symbolism of which is primarily reminiscent of a primitive fertility ritual? Let's be honest: how right in the head can you be to grab a fish by the tail, raise it up to eye level, tilt back your head and gobble the carcass down, before examining the inedible tail with a look that says 'what is all this about then?' Is that what we invented fire for, or why we learned to walk on two legs?

This damning criticism of Dutch cuisine begs the question of whether the Dutchman is indeed an unimaginative *eigenheimer*, a frugal masher who has no place in the world of fine dining. Many Dutch people will retort by saying that compared to countries where a sodden newspaper containing fish and chips, a king-size *Bratwurst* and a bucket of *Bier* or a portion of barbecue-charred meat pass for culinary masterpieces, things aren't that bad.

Even so, pointing out other barbarians does not exonerate us. There was indeed a time when most Dutch people did eat frugally. Simple, nutritious meals were the order of the day in many families without much money to spend. In many households, the menu was dictated by a weekly rhythm, sometimes in harmony with the church or the local butcher who displayed his wares on regular days – the expressions 'Wednesday mince day' and 'fish Friday' refer to this. An absolute starring role was reserved for the potato, which is not, by the way, a Dutch invention, but one that the Spaniards purloined from the Incas. It took some time to integrate, but from that point there was no holding back: the spud was rarely absent from the hot evening meal. And people have long been mashing food at the table, although it was not at all a general habit, despite what some self-appointed experts would have you believe.

Dining out was a rare pleasure for the Dutch, reserved for special occasions. In such cases they would visit a Chinese, Indonesian or Chinese-Indonesian restaurant. Not only because the choice was limited but also because the prices were low. These restaurants have been so familiar to the Dutch for decades that they are generally viewed as completely 'Dutch'.

However, times have changed. The increase in prosperity allowed the Dutch to expand their frontiers, and they didn't need to be asked twice, even if caution and frugality continued to prevail at first. The classic tale of Dutch people cramming their luggage with Dutch food on their first foreign holidays is true. 'You never know with foreign food,' my next-door neighbour once confided in me. Her distrust applied in particular to Italian olive oil – dodgy stuff, if I understood her right. She was taking no chances, and filled the car and caravan with tinned food, bags of potatoes and boxes of Norit. As the entire street waved them goodbye, our neighbours headed off into the unknown with their axles scraping the tarmac.

Since then, the Dutch have shaken off their fear. They travel the world, happily subjecting themselves to all manner of food poisoning. They spend a fortune on airline tickets to eat roasted grasshoppers in dubious markets next to open sewers and gain experience from cooks with the hygiene standards of fourteenth-century prison guards. They will try out big, juicy frogs, fresh snake, obscene-smelling durians, or bowls of greasy Tibetan butter tea. They eat, of course, with their hands and drink the tap water everywhere they go, as that is what the locals do. They crave Montezuma's Revenge, the Rangoon Runs, the Delhi Belly and the Suez Surprise, and they are not disappointed: they acquire all different kinds of diarrhoea at the same time and in their fevered dreams they see three wise men wearing turbans and their camels staring at a falling star in the shape of a giant cheese sandwich made with brown bread. Once safely home, they will tell the whole story down to the last detail to their friends, relatives, acquaintances and workmates, who walk away immediately – straight to the nearest travel agent.

At home too, the Dutch have greatly broadened their culinary horizons. Of course, during the winter they still regularly eat kale, endive *stamppot* with pieces of bacon, *hutspot* and sauerkraut – with *rockworst* indeed, which is actually called *rookworst*. And when it's possible to skate on natural ice, the stalls selling pea soup alongside the frozen ponds, creeks and canals are essential. However, the potato is facing stiff competition from the increasingly pushy rice and pasta, and separate starters, exotic main courses and adventurous salads which no one even knew existed two generations ago appear at the drop of a hat. This happens, for example, when a foreign guest arrives, licking his lips at the thought of trying meatballs, potatoes and sprouts or another typical Dutch dish. Unfortunately for the guest there's a good chance that the meatball will be served up a day later. The Dutchman's faith in traditional cuisine has not lapsed entirely, but he has simply made the old adage 'Variety is the spice of life' his own.

The retail business has made things easy for him. The supermarkets were no slouches in taking advantage of these new eating habits, and in fact they have brazenly paved the way by continually introducing new delicacies. The shelves were soon overflowing with exotic foods and titbits. And anything you can't find there can certainly be found in the Indonesian *tokos* and the many Turkish and Moroccan shops.

The idea that the Netherlands is a bastion of conservative culinary traditions, drenched in the familiar odour of sprouts, is just as misplaced as the idea that it's a good place for mountain walks. On the contrary, culinary innovations have not made inroads in any other western country as quickly as in the Netherlands. Once they had a little money in their pockets, Van Gogh's potato eaters quickly turned out to be culinary hedonists for whom no horizon was too distant.

The deluge of exotic restaurants bears this out. Over half of all Dutch restaurants offer foreign cuisine, and outside the home the Dutch eat 'foreign' more often than any other people. Ethiopia, Mongolia, Afghanistan, Tibet – you name the country and it will have a culinary outpost in one of the larger cities. When a new tribe is discovered deep in the Amazon, there's a good chance that they've already been running three restaurants in the centre of Amsterdam for years.

Is there, among all this exotic madness, anywhere you can still enjoy a classic Dutch menu? There certainly is. Not only are there specialist restaurants which would make any lover of mashed potato dishes feel at home, but also an increasing number of all-round establishments with dishes such as black pudding, *stamppot* with *rookworst* and a well of gravy, marrowfat peas, stewing steaks and semolina pudding on the menu. This reappraisal of grandma's cooking goes hand in glove with an urge to innovate. 'Exciting' Dutch cuisine is in, and the innovative chefs at trendy restaurants and the pioneering pancake-maker are both aware of the fact. The latter can be thanked for the un-surpassed liquorice pancake.

Increased interest is also enjoyed by the wealth of traditional regional dishes which can, without exaggeration, be said to be astonishing in a country as small as the Netherlands. More and more restaurants offer a local menu or use specialities of the region, with almost 'forgotten' products experiencing in turn a glorious revival.

This doesn't leave much over for the embittered Hollandolo-gists, you could say. Although guests from warmer countries may sometimes be taken aback by the early (by their standards) clos-ing times of many kitchens. Outside the big cities in particular, it's common for the chef to close up after ten o'clock. And of course, as a dyed-in-the-wool vegetarian you'd be better off in India, but compared to the rest of Europe the choice of vegetarian dishes is large. Even the authentic steak house sometimes takes the hun-gry vegetarian into account, the hospitable manager of such an establishment recently assured me: 'We've always got Quorn and that sort of rubbish here too.'

The fact remains, the quality of the food can disappoint. In order to avoid unpleasant surprises, there is a mountain of reading matter available to the gastronome, in which inspectors of diverse plumage explore the nation's restaurants. Michelin's critical researchers who are known for their severe judgements ('Tastes of rubber') rewarded over eighty Dutch restaurants with one or more stars in 2007.

Of course, the hot meal is not the only gateway to the culi-nary Netherlands. After all, the Dutch eat but one hot meal a day. Those wishing to penetrate deep into the heart of the national food culture must also partake of the bread-based meals. They may sound dull, but there's no shortage of variety. All shapes and sizes of bread are available at bakeries, from whiter-than-white through all shades of brown to almost black. Foreigners who find it hard to adapt to the typically thin Dutch sandwiches can fill their boots with a rich assortment of buns, rolls, currant buns, baguettes, croissants and both sweet and savoury pastries. And then you have the pitch-black Frisian rye bread, a formidable array of crackers and the pride of every breakfast table: *ontbijtkoek*, a type of breakfast cake. If you'd prefer something ready-made outside the home, there are plenty of places where you can buy a fashionable low-calorie baguette or ciabatta with a pile of green fodder and other healthy ingredients. An essential outing for the amateur anthropologist is a visit to a snack bar, cafeteria or such well-known establishments as *Broodje van Kootje* in Amsterdam, where traditional dishes such as the *broodje kroket*, the *uitsmijter*, the cheese roll and the inseparable glass of milk grace the bill of fare.

Dairy produce, and cheese in particular, is as famous a Dutch symbol as the clog, the windmill and the tulip. It's no wonder, either, as the Dutch are by far the greatest exporters of cheese in the world. They are not mockingly called *kaaskop* (cheese-head) in Belgium for nothing, after the mould in which the famous round Edam cheese is made. Names like Edam and Gouda are music to the ears of cheese lovers worldwide, even if they have no idea how to pronounce them.

However, these two towns are just the tip of the national cheese mountain. The enthusiastic cheese pilgrim wishing to explore the country through local cheese specialities will be kept busy for at least a couple of weeks. Leiden (cumin cheese), Friesland (clove cheese), Texel (cheese made with unpasteurised milk)

– these are just a few of the many compulsory stops on a cheese odyssey, which of course has to end up at the famous cheese market in Alkmaar. Once there, the exhausted pilgrim can allow himself to be carried away by a pair of trotting cheese carriers.

The flourishing dairy sector has several irons in the fire: the Netherlands is also the biggest exporter of butter and milk powder. In shops and supermarkets all over the world, black and white cows stare at shoppers from countless packages and cans. In a number of ways, the cow is a national mascot, although the Dutchman is no stranger to a certain hypocrisy in this regard. He also maintains a cruel, animal-unfriendly factory farming business that takes the lives of 1.5 million calves every year, most of whom have never known the green, grassy meadows. The Dutch, who are up in arms in great numbers at the first suspicion of animal suffering and can become deeply scandalised by the dismal lot of the dogs bred for meat in Korea, don't lose any sleep over it. Those representing the interests of the industry speak soothingly of 'an honest piece of meat'. There are few who ask what exactly is honest about it.

One last special contribution by the dairy world to global civilisation is *vla*, a custard-like dessert. Walk around a supermarket and the conclusion is unavoidable: the Netherlands is a dessert paradise. Chocolate *vla*, caramel *vla*, vanilla *vla*, banana *vla*, strawberry *vla*, Ajax *vla* – the refrigerator is bursting with the colourful sweetness. The Dutch are mad about it, but many foreigners are not enamoured with the stuff. Too exotic, too chemical and in particular, too sweet.

Many visitors receive a tremendous culture shock for the same reasons when they first encounter the sandwich fillings and spreads. The unusually comprehensive Dutch breakfast is renowned, but a modest plateful of *hagelslag* (chocolate sprinkles) is enough to ruin the appetites of most foreigners for hours. And that's before they come across the chocolate flakes, chocolate spread, jam, apple syrup and coconut slices on the breakfast table. In spite of the popularity of the great Dutch painters, they will never understand the art of decorating bread. They are more likely to associate the sickly spreads with children's parties than serious food.

However, the Dutch have their own ideas about children's parties. In comparison with the sugariness that is served up on these occasions, the sandwich spreads are but child's play. Although he barely realises it, the Dutchman is born with a sweet tooth. Typically, he will brighten up every holiday occasion with his own sweet specialities. The Easter *stollen*, Christmas chocolate wreaths, apple turnovers and *oliebollen* sell like hot cakes and by early December the shelves are sagging under the weight of the typical Sinterklaas fare and its wonderful symbolism: chocolate letters, spice nuts, spiced biscuits, gingerbread, chocolate coins, candies and marzipan.

To many foreigners, the Dutch sweet tin is a Pandora's Box. Typical native delicacies such as the treacle waffle, the spiced biscuit and the *Haagse hopje* caramel elicit at best a dutiful enthusiasm, while others lead to bewilderment and unconcealed disgust. The Dutch derive endless amusement from the blend of horror and distrust which overcomes the foreigner on eating a *dropje* liquorice sweet. They themselves are addicted to the black gold, though it reminds the rest of the world more of a medicine – which it originally was, including in the Netherlands. 'Are you trying to poison me?' is the typical response. Oh, not really, replies the Dutch person, who is never averse to explaining that one has to *learn* to enjoy sweets. You'll have to bite the bullet, then, or you'll remain a *drop*-out in the Netherlands. However, the advice rarely helps. Even the introduction of the *dropshot*, a liqueur with twenty percent alcohol, made little difference.

Foreigners in need of a drink can enjoy the brews of the Heineken company, the brewery which has given the Netherlands its status of beer nation. The company is so famous that a great many foreigners can pronounce its name without difficulty. Heineken is also the world's largest exporter of beer and it is consumed in 170 countries.

A beverage that is more typically Dutch than beer is *jenever*, the spirit based on grain alcohol. The first distillery in the world opened its gates in Amsterdam in the sixteenth century. It was Schiedam, though, that would become the *jenever* capital. At one point the city was home to over four-hundred *jenever* distilleries. Travellers' publications indicate that the aroma of fermenting malt and juniper berries filled the streets in previous centuries. The grain needed for its manufacture was ground in twenty gigantic mills, five of which have survived the ravages of time.

In terms of popularity, *jenever* could never match the success of Heineken, although the English word 'gin' – derived from *jenever*, as 'brandy' is derived from *brandewijn* – demonstrates that it was drunk regularly in other countries. These days, as a typical 'old man's drink', *jenever* struggles with an image problem that is hard to shake off. However, the distillers have also long produced all kinds of liqueurs and, these days, even vodka; drinks which are popular both in the Netherlands and abroad.

In recent times, the Netherlands has unleashed another alcoholic surprise for the curious culinary tourist: wine. Many will deem this insane or at least furrow their brows at the suggestion, but nevertheless a new wine nation is being established in the polders. Due to the lack of sunlight, the winegrowers sometimes have to help the process along by adding sugar to achieve the required alcohol level, for instance, but even bitter Hollandologists have to admit that the products are now of a reasonable quality. The Dutch share of European production is still very modest, but the number of vineyards is growing fast.

However, there is a dark side to this sterling alcoholic tradition. The Dutch youth are proud leaders in the European 'alcohol consumption between tricycle and moped' competition. Over half of fifteen-year-olds seem to drink as much as the adults, although not in their company. The government recently pledged to tackle this abuse, but an additional problem is that some of the young people enjoy a tipple in what they call a *zuipkeet* (booze shed). These are self-built huts, sheds or parts of a greenhouse in which teenagers practice the noble art of *comazuipen* – drinking almost up to the point of falling over, or just beyond it, of course.

These 'beer dens' are flourishing especially in the Dutch Bible Belt. In this region, parents would rather their offspring did not go to public establishments where 'un-Christian' music is made. Meanwhile, the fact that their children drink themselves into a stupor in a shed in the back garden is no problem. The rural local authorities distinguish themselves with their unique interpretation of the famous tolerance formula, which has enabled the existence of coffeeshops in the towns.

One interesting detail is that in some areas, the youngsters have developed their own drinks with which to do themselves in. The most delightful local speciality is that of the Reformed fishing village of Urk, the jewel of the Bible Belt, where according to a renowned saying, they 'pray just as much as they drink'. The youth of Urk swear by the cheeky *Jezusklapper* (Jesus slammer), a mixture of whisky, Stroh rum, Sambuca, Martini, Jägermeister and lemon *jenever*. It is not known whether a few glasses enable you to walk on water.

The Netherlands as a supplier of alcohol and a booze shed for teenagers. It is nothing to be proud of, but it may be of some comfort to the Hollandologists who find Dutch cuisine utterly revolting. It's not all that bad after a few jars.

MoRE tHAN CLoG-DANCiNG

Cultural highlights of the Low Countries

Few people will be surprised to learn that there's more to cultural life in the Netherlands than clog-dancing and barrel organs, more even than Rembrandt and Van Gogh. Though more will be surprised that the country is overflowing with cultural expression. The Netherlands is teeming with museums, cultural centres and libraries. Theatre, dance, music and cabaret groups. Gifted soloists in a variety of fields. And large and small events and festivals. Countless Dutch artists perform all over the world and a range of groups – from the Concertgebouworkest to the Nationale Ballet – enjoy great international acclaim, not least because of their artistic individuality. There are countries with fewer cultural treats.

The Netherlands also enjoy international acclaim in the fields of architecture and design. Whether industrial design or clothing design, its praises are regularly sung worldwide under the collective name of 'Dutch design'.

Even so, the international image of Dutch culture is still dominated by a handful of painters who kicked the bucket centuries ago. Rembrandt and Van Gogh, in particular, belong to the select group of *IBNers*, the International Dutch Celebrities. The museums in which one can admire their work are first-class tourist attractions – the Rijksmuseum and the Van Gogh Museum in Amsterdam especially. Temporary exhibitions of their work cause ticket office queues worldwide. The work of the two greats is rarely sold, but when it is, staggering amounts of money change hands.

It's far less well-known that these painters only attained icon status posthumously. Even during the Golden Age, the heyday of painting when not only Rembrandt but also Johannes Vermeer, Frans Hals, Jan Steen, Jacob van Ruysdael, Pieter de Hoogh and dozens of others gained their fame, the artists were seen primarily as artisans. Certainly, the prosperity of the seventeenth century provided the artist with a much-appreciated stage. Inventors, designers, scientists and other creative spirits also profited from the favourable economic climate – the microscope, the telescope, the pendulum clock and the fire hose are all examples of the stream of innovations which sprouted from the polder soil during this period. Wealthy merchants and other members of the urban elite were keen to be immortalised by Rembrandt and his contemporaries. But the esteem enjoyed by the artists rested primarily on their ability to portray their client to his greater honour and glory. If the canvas was not to the patron's liking it was cast aside thoughtlessly, or the artist might even fall from grace.

The sad fortunes of perhaps the most famous painting in the world, Rembrandt's *Nightwatch,* is a salient example of this. It is what is known as a militia piece, a depiction of a company of Amsterdam militia – a civil guard of mainly well-heeled gentlemen. The painting was commissioned by the men themselves and intended for the building at which they convened. Every militia had group portraits on the walls of their clubhouses. Customarily, they were named after the officers who took up prominent positions within the paintings: *Het korporaalschap van kapitein Frans Banning Cocq en luitenant Willem van Ruytenburgh* is its full title. It acquired the title of *The Nightwatch* after it became darker due to the discolouration of the varnish. Rembrandt worked on the vast canvas from 1638 to 1642, probably under a lean-to in the garden of his Amsterdam home, now the Rembrandt House Museum.

These days, the painting is admired for its spectacular dynamics and light and shadow play. However, the men of the militia were not at all happy with this modernism. They were profoundly disappointed with the result. What had that madman Rembrandt done? What kind of chaotic tableau was this? Why weren't the brave gentlemen sitting neatly in a row, or enjoying their traditional banquet, as the rules of the popular genre dictated? Several of the militia men were so peeved that they refused to pay the agreed sum of a hundred guilders.

It was to be a harbinger of even greater calamity to come. In 1715, the painting was moved from the militia clubhouse to the city hall of Amsterdam, the proud bastion of government that had been completed fifty years before. The city fathers had a nice spot in mind, neatly positioned between two windows, but on arrival it turned out the painting didn't fit: it was too big. What could be done? You can picture the distress: two porters in grey dust jackets lean the painting against the wall and scratch their heads. But no matter how long they look at it, the painting doesn't get any smaller. 'What possesses these crazy artists to make these paintings so big all the time?' one says. That doesn't help either. As it's nearly time for their coffee break, the handymen decide they should take action. One of them takes out his Stanley knife and cuts strips off all sides of the canvas, even taking some sixty centimetres off one side. Three meticulously-depicted figures disappear into the bin along with these strips. There you go.

Rembrandt, who died in 1669, had less than a positive experience with the new city hall when alive, too. In 1656, his bankruptcy was declared in the yet-unfinished building. Around the same time, commissions for the decoration of the immense *Burgerzaal* of the city hall passed him by. He had to watch, gnashing his teeth, as his former student Govert Flinck was put to work. Only when Flinck died before completing his commission was Rembrandt called on to provide a painting. It was to be an ode to the Batavian revolt which bloodied the nose of the proud Roman legions in the first century AD. It was up to Rembrandt to make the brave ancestors shine.

Just like *The Nightwatch*, Rembrandt's *The Conspiracy of the Batavians* did not meet with the critics' approval. The city fathers felt the Batavians, to whom they compared themselves, were too small – much too small. These people weren't heroes, they were Lilliputians. And what about their leader, Julius Civilis? Was this one-eyed oddball supposed to be a perfect, heroic leader? Once again, the Stanley knife was unsheathed, only this time it was brandished by Rembrandt himself, after he and his Batavians were shown the door. As the massive canvas was unsaleable, he cut out the middle section. This now hangs in the National-museum in Stockholm and is popularly called *The Nightwatch of the North*.

Problems with clients and financial mismanagement meant the initially burgeoning career of Rembrandt, the miller's son, would take a negative turn. After his death, he was buried in a simple unmarked grave in the Westerkerk in Amsterdam, its exact location unknown. This has been the sad fate of many a Dutch icon: Hans Brinker turns out never to have existed and the country's most famous artist is nowhere to be found.

Rembrandt was no exception. Many of his contemporaries who were celebrated with hindsight had great difficulty keeping their heads above water although there was a market for their work. As well as the moneyed classes, private individuals were also interested in art. Foreign visitors in the seventeenth century were amazed to see paintings on the walls of normal homes and even farmhouses. This was only possible because the prices were generally low. Landscapes in particular were highly affordable – the artists made hardly any money out of them.

Rembrandt's most famous contemporaries, Frans Hals and Johannes Vermeer, were continually in financial problems. Hals regularly had to appear in court because of his debts to his baker, his butcher and his cobbler in succession. He settled the baker's bill with a number of paintings. He survived on handouts in the later years of his life, although he continued to paint.

Vermeer also got into trouble with his baker. His work was hung on the bakery wall, as security against his debt of 617 guilders. He died poor and unknown, leaving a wife, eleven children and a colossal debt. If an artist must suffer in order to perform great works, the famous Dutch painters are perfect examples.

The great modern artist Vincent van Gogh (1853-1890) fits seamlessly into this sad tradition. He was so poor that he suffered regularly from malnutrition. Furthermore, he was a sensitive, lonely and sometimes desperate man. In 1888 he cut off part of his left ear with a razor following an argument with his friend, the French artist Paul Gauguin. Two years later he took his own life. He had been able to sell just one of his hundreds of paintings, and according to some experts he never sold one. Nowadays, astronomical sums are paid for these works and Van Gogh is considered to be a founder of twentieth-century art.

Happily, there is a lot less suffering in the world of modern-day Dutch art and culture. The greatest sufferers are perhaps the painters, as their role is considerably more modest than in the past. The most talked-about achievements these days are those in the field of architecture. With architects such as Rem Koolhaas and Ben van Berkel at the forefront, the Netherlands acquired a reputation as a Mecca of modern architecture at the end of the last century. The adoration for the adventurous Dutch experiments, both home and abroad, were reflected in the honorary tile of 'Superdutch'. But the Netherlands would not be the Netherlands if people did not wonder aloud whether this compliment was deserved. After all, weren't traditional designs becoming more common in the construction of housing? However, the fact remains that unusual structures are built in the Netherlands with clockwork regularity, from offices and museums to railway stations and waterworks.

That's a good thing too, because quite a few suburbs of unprecedented dreary uniformity have surreptitiously been laid out in the polders in recent times. Due to the growth in population, functionality became predominant, as was the case in the garden cities founded soon after the Second World War to afford labourers and other 'normal' people decent living quarters. This philosophy won the garden cities pride of place in twentieth-century architecture, but the modern suburbs are unlikely to receive the same accolades. They are generally referred to as 'littering' the landscape, like the mammoth concrete stores and flat blocks of the 'seventies ('vending machines') which in the eyes of many brought about a dramatic 'degeneration' of the cities.

The surprising versatility and strong architectural tradition has made the Netherlands a paradise for architecture enthusiasts. The densely-sown historical city centres, the old fortified towns and the romantic farmhouses with their traditional pollard willows in front of the door invariably fire the tourist's imagination. Architectural pilgrims are delighted to find architectural styles which are hardly seen outside the Netherlands, such as the work of the great twentieth-century architect Hendrik Berlage, the *Amsterdamse School* and *De Stijl*.

It's not surprising that design is in the Dutch blood: almost the whole country was developed at the drawing board. This is also borne out by the international furore surrounding the designers with their inventive 'Dutch design'. The character of Dutch design is practical, simple, recognisable and pioneering, whether you are talking about letterboxes, furniture, postage stamps or the Dutch banknotes, now sadly vanquished by the vulgar euro. All attract worldwide interest. Some experts even dig up the term 'model country' to classify the Dutch design tradition. There's no such excitement in the Netherlands itself. The down-to-earth designs are quickly dubbed 'very normal' in a typically restrained manner.

One area in which Dutch designers have long been the 'guide' is that of road signs. The best examples are the signs at Schiphol, the first airport to realise the importance of clear signage. The system designed by Bureau Mijksenaar was also implemented at the three New York airports. The American metropolis' underground rail system was signposted by Bob Noorda, who is also responsible for the underground systems in São Paulo and Milan.

The unstoppable rise of Dutch fashion design has been a painful one for the moral censors who have painted the Dutch as the worst-dressed mammals of all time; the Dutchman's informal style can apparently be traced directly back to the bearskins of the Batavians and the dolmen builders. Dutch fashion designers are in demand worldwide for their creativity and ability to design eyecatching but practical clothes. A remarkable number of Dutch people work for leading international brands, while Dutch brands are also popular abroad.

Modern successes of Dutch design like the Maxi-Cosi, the Bugaboo (both modes of transport for children) and the Heineken Beertender are part of a long tradition of which showpieces such as the Dutch toilet, the Daffodil with its revolutionary automatic gearbox – the *pientere pookje* or smart gearstick – and the Fokker F27 Friendship and its successors still excite aficionados. Deserving of an honourable mention is Philips, the Eindhoven electronics company which has been pumping out elegant inventions since the Russian tsar ordered fifty thousand light bulbs in 1898. In 1928, the company demonstrated a television set, twenty years before the medium was introduced in the Netherlands. Later, it contributed to the development of the radio and – to the joy of all Dutch people – the dynamo-powered bicycle lamp. Its electric shaver, called Philishave, became world-famous as did the audio cassette, the home video cassette system, the compact disc and a range of medical systems.

Another thing that brought joy to all Dutch people was the Senseo, introduced in 2001: a stylish coffee maker that is fed ingenious 'coffee pads' and was designed in partnership with the coffee baron, Douwe Egberts. The Senseo enjoys unprecedented popularity. It's no wonder, as the machine forms an essential contribution to Dutch culture. Thanks to this attractive appliance, the Dutch are now assured for years to come of an excellent cup of coffee, which can be enjoyed with the traditional *gezelligheid*. Along with a biscuit, of course.

Sources cited

Quotations and references to previous travellers have been extracted from:

Amicis, Edmondo de, *Nederland en zijn bewoners*, Veen, Utrecht/Antwerpen, 1985.

Dodge, Mary Mapes, *Hans Brinker or The Silver Skates: A Story of Life In Holland*, Charles Scribner's Sons, New York, 1905.

Stipriaan, René van (compiler), *Achter de dijken – Buitenlandse schrijvers over Nederland*, Prometheus, Amsterdam, 1997.

Stott, Annette, *Holland Mania – The Unknown Dutch Period in American Art and Culture*, The Overlook Press, Woodstock, 1998.

Strien, Kees van, *De Ontdekking van de Nederlanden – Britse en Franse reizigers in Holland en Vlaanderen, 1750-1795*, Het Spectrum, Utrecht, 2001.